ALWAYS BUILDING
THE PROGRAMMABLE ENVIRONMENT

JIM LONG
JENNIFER MAGNOLFI
LOIS MAASSEN

HERMAN MILLER CREATIVE OFFICE

©2008 Herman Miller, Inc., Zeeland, Michigan 49464
Printed in U.S.A. on recycled paper

HermanMiller.com and HMConvia.com

ISBN 978-0-9816934-0-8

This book marks a milestone in the development of a new idea for Herman Miller. It results from the contributions of a network of people, both inside and outside the company, thinkers, innovators, technologists, and practitioners who are keenly interested in more sustainable built environments.

We'd particularly like to acknowledge the work of our colleagues in the Herman Miller Creative Office, who first described and tested "Project Purple," a path to the promise of programmable environments.

Special thanks to the Purple Design Concept Team, comprising Danny Hillis and Bran Ferren, founding partners of Applied Minds, Inc., and Sheila Kennedy, founding partner of Kennedy & Violich Architecture, LTD. Their work and insight drove the first interpretation of these ideas. Further, we thank Ayse Birsel, co-principal of Birsel+Seck, for her special contributions to the early product concepts.

We thank the Convia™ business team for contributing information for this book and for taking a foundation for programmable environments into the marketplace.

All of these and many more contributors are advocates for change in the way in which the built environment is planned, designed, constructed, and used. We are grateful to be their representatives in putting these ideas into print.

CONTENTS

p.9 **INTRODUCTION**

p.20 **THE PROMISE**
OF PROGRAMMABLE ENVIRONMENTS
Built environments are out of sync with the change required in our economy and society; they don't take advantage of technology to be responsive either to human needs or to demands for sustainability. Five areas of change help us see a new direction for the built environment.

p.50 **OUR EXPLORATION**
OF PROGRAMMABILITY
The Herman Miller Creative Office saw potential for new value in making buildings less rigid and more sustainable. Finding that space division and utility delivery caused rigidity, we set about to find ways to apply modularity and programmability as two paths to flexibility.

p.68 **ACHIEVING THE PROMISE**
OF PROGRAMMABILITY
Given our exploration, we've identified fundamental design principles and thought about how programmable environments will be created and experienced. We think these environments will make people's lives better. We invite others to explore, invent, implement, and learn along with us.

p.91 **FURTHER READING**

INTRODUCTION

In the United States more than 824,000 office buildings hold more than 12 billion square feet. More than 213,000 enclosed and strip malls add another 7 billion square feet; 129,000 health care buildings add 3 billion square feet more. In 2006 alone, the last year reported, $544 billion was spent on commercial construction projects. From any perspective this is economically compelling. There are very few businesses that don't participate in some way in the construction, operation, and use of the built environment. Retail businesses measure their performance in spatial terms—dollars of sales per square foot. Vice presidents of corporate real estate are endlessly searching for measures for the productivity of their investments in offices. It is obvious that space and business are inextricably linked. What is not obvious, and what is surprising, is how poorly business builds and uses space. The National Institute of Building Sciences, which tracks both commercial and residential construction, quotes a Construction Industry Institute estimate of "up to 57 percent non-value added effort or waste in our current business models. This means the industry may waste over $600 billion each year." On the demand side the problem is equally dire, as described in *Business Week*:

> Working anywhere but work is causing a vast emptying out in corporate-land. About 60 percent of the office space that companies pay so dearly for is now a dead zone of darkened doorways and wasting cubes. "Imagine if a factory had a utilization rate of 40 percent," says Mark Golan, vice president for worldwide real estate and workplace resources at Cisco Systems, Inc.

Huge waste in the construction process that provides space that ultimately doesn't even get used—from any perspective this is a big problem.

Whether the organization is service or manufacturing, profit or not-for-profit, public or private, its operations intersect with design in solving the problems of its use of space. So this is a business book because it is about a business problem, but it is a design book because design is the source of the solution.

Charles Eames said, in the early 70s, "Design depends largely on constraints." Game developer Dino Dini elaborates: "Design is simply the management of constraints, and the choice of which constraints are nonnegotiable is crucial." Solving the problem of space requires a reevaluation of the negotiability of constraints. What once seemed crucial may no longer be so, and what is crucial now may be entirely new.

One of those new constraints is a word that wasn't even known when many of the buildings we see today were built: sustainability. By many measures sustainability, or green building, has yet to have a significant effect on the way in which we build, operate and occupy the built environment. But we believe it will, and so it provides the foundation for our reevaluation of the design constraints in the problem of space.

We have found a way to think about the interiors of commercial space that is aligned with the constraints of the beginning of the 21st century. Our ideas stand on the shoulders of the work of inventors, architects, designers, and thinkers from around the world. The terms coined to describe the future of place point toward, but never fully capture, what a sustainable built environment will be. *Ubiquitous computing, ambient intelligence, flexible architecture, adaptive architecture, kinetic structures, smart architecture, intelligent buildings, responsive architecture*—these are all different ways to describe very similar phenomena. We have chosen to call our idea *programmable environments*.

What we describe accepts the work that has gone before as a fundamental part of our view. Environments will be imbued with intelligence. Although the full meaning of that is yet to be worked out, we do know we will want that intelligence to serve; to us that means it must be programmable. But it is not just the intelligence that is programmed, it is the whole of the environment.

A programmable environment is as much about the creation and management of space as it is about the intelligence that is in it; it is an environment for people to occupy, to meet, to educate, to heal, to worship, and to enjoy one another's company.

Throughout this discussion, we intend the larger meaning of the word *program*: a plan of action to meet a goal. We want to create environments with which we can interact to achieve our goals. We want programmable environments. Our primary and nonnegotiable design constraint is sustainability.

This book is the story of the development of the idea of programmable environments and how that idea has generated new product ideas. Our goal is to change how buildings are designed, built, managed, and used. We know that can only happen one building and one day at a time, with many hands and minds at work on the problem. This is our start.

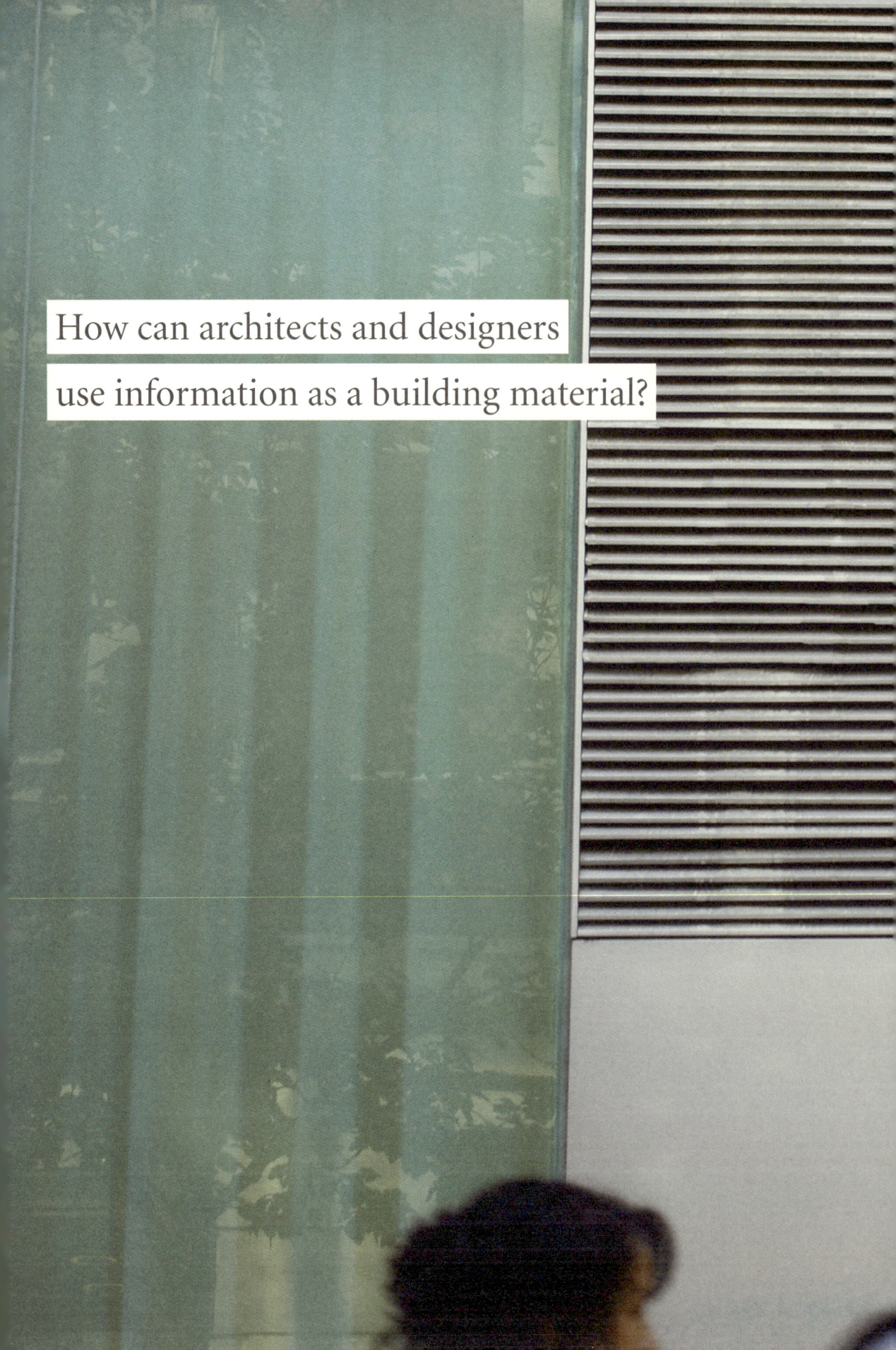

How can architects and designers use information as a building material?

How can the construction process be made easier and less costly through embedded technology?

How can our environments be adaptable—even by the people who use them—after they're built?

How can technology reinvent our environments?

Observing the digital transformation of society teaches us a great deal. We have framed a vision of the future where information technology and distributed computing will not only permeate our work and daily experiences, but will also constitute the very makeup of our built environment. This will create tremendous opportunities for solving one of the long-standing problems in buildings as we know them—the costly and time-consuming effort required to accommodate change.

Our buildings are at odds with the notion of change. Fixed utilities, unforgiving infrastructure, rigid materials, and lack of control inhibit our ability to affect our surroundings. Buildings allow us only to be passive participants in their use. But what we require changes, and our inability to change the environment leads to its obsolescence.

The process of designing a building or interior environment is imbued with flexibility. It is a dynamic dialog between designer and artifact influenced by the requirements and values of all stakeholders. Flexibility, however, disappears once construction begins. The efficiency of construction and the economics of the overall process hinge on the design being frozen in time, casting change as an enemy of budgets and schedules. In the end, the space as built constitutes the final design. The building becomes a static expression of a set of requirements that began to change before the first occupant moved in.

New technologies can resolve the conflict between the freedom and interactivity of the design process and the static environments the process generates. It is becoming possible for buildings to change more efficiently and gracefully. Materials are becoming less rigid. Infrastructures are becoming more modular, consequently more suited for change. And control has the potential to be distributed in ways that allow design processes to become a part of the use and operation of a building.

The development and application of this technology requires innovation in all aspects of building design, construction, operation,

"We shape our buildings, and afterwards our buildings shape us."
–Winston Churchill, 1943

"We become what we behold. We shape our tools and then our tools shape us."
–Marshall McCluhan, 1964

and use. We believe this innovation in programmability is the pathway to sustainability in the built environment.

The programmable environment recognizes the generative potential of digital technology to create both form and compelling experiences. Digital technology must become an intrinsic component of the built environment, permeating the building and transforming its architecture from a design result into a design medium. Historically, inhabitants have accepted and adapted to their built environments. In contrast, programmable environments adapt to their occupants. As a design medium, the programmable environment affords opportunities for design engagement with all of its stakeholders.

This idea describes environments that are sustainable because they are designed for change, that at any moment are statements of our aspirations, that give form to the values driving society's development and progress. A programmable environment invites a new design paradigm charged with hope and innovation.

A NEW DESIGN MEDIUM
The notion of design medium applies to the technology itself, which allows designers of programmable environments to do things differently than previously possible. It also refers to the opportunities for innovation in the business practices of those involved in the design, building, operation, and use of programmable environments—understood as the things organizations do to run their businesses.

EVIDENCE OF POTENTIAL

	DIAGNOSTIC INFORMATION	PERFORMANCE DATA	PERSONALIZED SETTINGS	INTERCONNECTIVITY WITH DIGITAL DEVICES
🚗	✓	✓	✓	✓
🏛	?	?	?	?

The promise that technology offers our buildings is already evident in our cars—which we treat as mobile personal habitats. If cars can remember the comfort settings each driver prefers, why can't a building? If a car can provide diagnostic information to a mechanic, why can't a building provide the same to a facility manager? If a car can provide feedback that helps a driver improve her gas mileage, why can't a building help people use it better?

This analogy points us in the right direction, but what we envision reaches much further. Cars simply enable their drivers to use controls more conveniently, to take care of and use well the existing machine. You can't move the heat vents, create a different signal (a sound instead of a light) that your tires need air, update the styling, or change your car into a boat when you reach the ocean. A car with that kind of adaptability would come from a radical reinvention of an entire industry—which is what we propose for design and construction.

THE DEMAND FOR A NEW ARCHITECTURE

Changes in technology, behavior, and expectations are converging in the built environment, creating opportunity, demanding new architecture, and challenging us to figure out how to provide it.

Since at least 1956, when Alison and Peter Smithson introduced their House of the Future, architects, designers, and technologists around the world have been trying to understand the potential of technology in the built environment. Today, those efforts appear in sustainable architecture, intelligent buildings, various experiments that add computing to space, developments that merge media and architecture, and a host of other nascent movements and projects.

In 1956, much of this speculative and future-looking work was infused with optimism; now there is urgency. Concern about resource consumption and ecological impact is widespread, and construction and buildings play a major role. David Harris, president of the National Institute of Building Sciences, writes, "The construction industry is in the middle of a growing crisis worldwide," noting that 40 percent of the world's raw materials are consumed by buildings, and buildings use 40 percent of the world's energy.

There are, at the same time, exciting possibilities for change. Architect Mike Pearce, in collaboration with Arup Associates, designed and built the Eastgate Centre, a mid-rise building in Zimbabwe that uses only 10 percent of the energy of comparable buildings of traditional design. The building mimics the self-cooling mounds built by termites in the Zimbabwe wild. And the Institute for the Future speculates, "High-powered computing capability will be embedded in our physical environment, in living things, medicine, walls, furniture, garments, tools, utensils, and toys. We'll be able to interact with information in place as naturally as we interact now with physical things, which will become increasingly less passive, and more active."

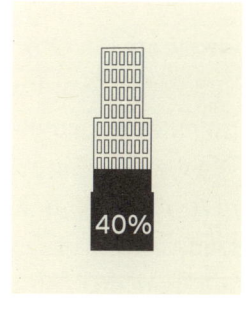

CONSUMPTION OF ENERGY AND MATERIALS
Forty percent of the world's raw materials are consumed by buildings, and buildings use 40 percent of the world's energy.

HOUSE OF THE FUTURE
Designed for the *Daily Mail* Ideal Home Show in 1956 by British architects Alison and Peter Smithson, the house included a table that rose from the floor to coffee or dining height, a shower that blasted the user with warm air, and a self-cleaning bath.

Our interest is in designing, building, and using the built environment. Our particular focus is the interior spaces of buildings—how they will change, how they can be better, how they can deliver what occupants need and do so more efficiently. What we need are new ways of seeing the world and different ways of thinking about how we interact with our environments. Here are five areas of change that provide some of these perspectives. While neither comprehensive nor conclusive, they provoke new ideas and lead to different ways of thinking.

Toward efficient, sustainable construction

The global construction industry employs more than 100 million people and an annual investment estimated at $4.6 trillion. Of that, the Construction Industry Institute estimates "up to 57 percent non-value-added effort or waste"; vacant buildings and empty offices suggest underutilization. Yet the amount of commercial space continues to grow. Since 1950 the amount of commercial space per capita in the U.S. has grown from 183 to 268 square feet per person—an increase of close to 50 percent.

The costs of operating and owning a building are high, in both financial and environmental terms. Commercial buildings in the U.S. account for nearly 18 percent of energy consumption, including nearly 33 percent of all electricity. Costs compound as occupants come and go, a building's use changes, and new technologies are introduced and layered in; the building and its systems become more complex and more difficult to support and maintain.

Building obsolescence is signaled by the proliferation of "for lease" signs in our business parks, downtowns, and strip malls—while new construction goes up alongside. In the U.S. alone, nearly 50,000 commercial buildings are demolished each year, adding to nearly 150 million tons of construction and demolition waste that is difficult to reclaim or recycle.

DEMOLITION ADDS TO LANDFILL
The nearly 50,000 commercial buildings demolished each year in the U.S. produce nearly 150 million tons of construction and demolition waste each year.

"Sustainability is never a static goal. It can only be a process."
–Bruce Sterling

LEARNING FROM NATURE
The Eastgate Centre is cooled without conventional air conditioning through biomimicry. Termites in Zimbabwe open and close ventilation passages throughout the day, using convection currents to keep the interior of their enormous mounds at a constant temperature. Breezes are directed into the cool mud below the mound during the heat of the day; those passages are closed at night to preserve the heat retained in the mound. The Eastgate Centre reinterprets the same principles through its application of vents, ducts, exhaust ports, and chimneys.

There is significant work underway to address these issues of expense and environmental impact. The National Institute of Building Sciences, Lean Construction Institute, and the U.S. Green Building Council approach the same issues from different perspectives. Better design informatics, like Building Information Modeling, make it possible to foresee and correct problems before construction starts. The lean manufacturing principles popularized by Toyota are equally applicable to construction. Architects, engineers, and design professionals are clearly showing interest in and understanding the value of green building practices, although they are still not widely adopted in the industry at large.

The inefficiencies of the fragmentation of the design and construction process evoked a more radical response from Dennis Kaspori, who calls for "open source architecture." In contrast with the hierarchical "cathedral model," with the "autonomous genius of the chief designer" at the top, he calls for a "bazaar model… based on cooperation. It conforms to the network logic of an effective distribution of ideas, as a result of which these ideas can be tested in different situations and improved. It makes use of the 'swarm intelligence' of a large group of users and/or developers."

The convergence of all of these streams of thought—on eliminating waste from both the means and the ends of construction—suggests the potential for far-reaching change in how buildings are designed, created, and used.

GROWTH IN GREEN BUILDING
Since the launch of the U.S. Green Building Council in the late 1990s, the growth in membership and registered projects has been extraordinary: from 533 accredited professionals in 2000 to 20,900 in 2006; from roughly 25 registered projects in 2000 to nearly 700 in 2006. Nevertheless, McGraw-Hill Construction estimates that only 5 to 10 percent of nonresidential construction starts in 2010 will be designed using green principles.

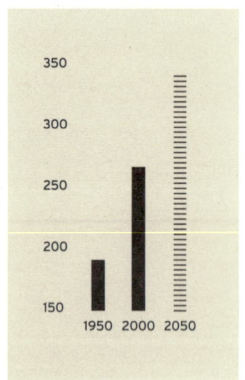

SPACE PER CAPITA INCREASES
Since 1950 the amount of commercial space per capita in the United States has grown from 183 square feet per person to 268 square feet per person–an increase of close to 50 percent. At this rate of growth there will be 350 square feet of commercial space per person by 2050.

CATHEDRAL

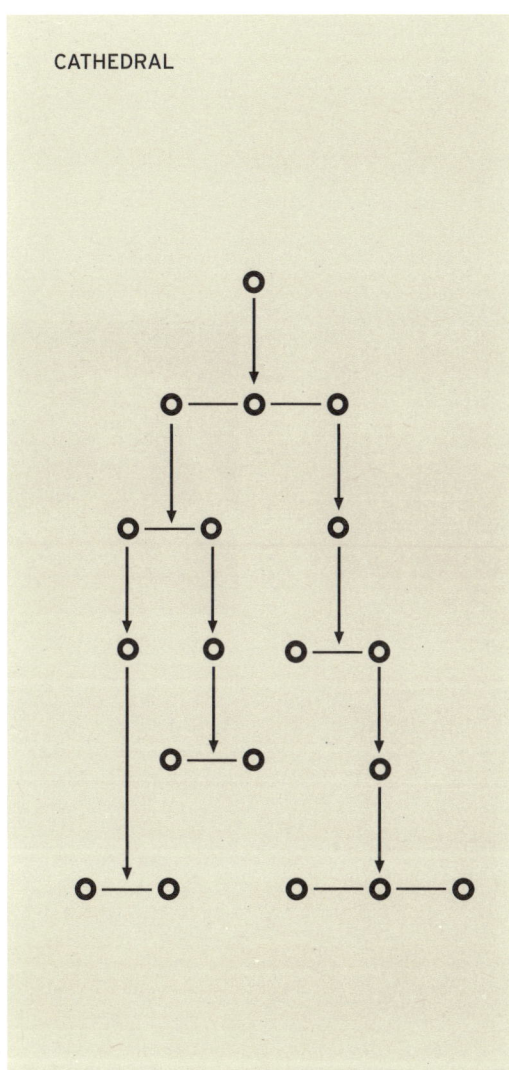

COLLABORATIVE

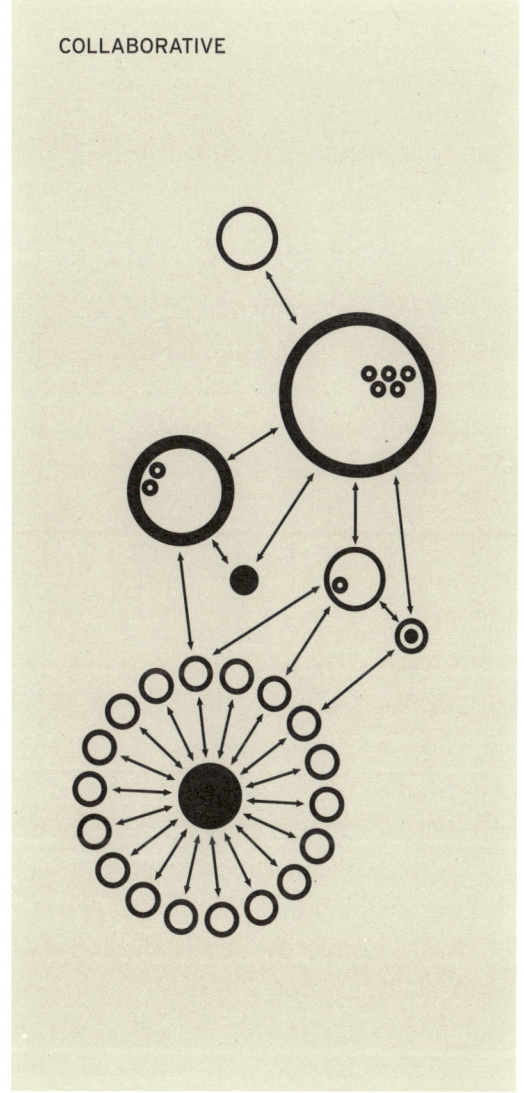

NEW COLLABORATIVE MODELS
"Examples of collaborative practices can be found in art and in software engineering. They offer an alternative model in which innovation is achieved through the active participation of all parties. Ideas and products are no longer developed in a closed production process organized around the autonomy of the artist or the company, but evolve out of the pragmatism of usage. That is the motor of innovation."

—Dennis Kaspori,
*A Communism of Ideas:
Towards an Architectural
Open Source Practice*

Toward smart things in smart buildings

Technology and architecture have a long symbiotic relationship, in which advances in one field enable or demand changes in the other. Electric power, elevators, new materials, computer-based modeling of innovative structures: These all opened new possibilities for buildings. Changes in architecture and the economics and culture that often drive them have required new technologies. Large-scale engineering and materials innovation have resulted, as well as things as simple as fire alarms, illuminated exit signs, PA systems, security cameras, and sprinkling systems.

Everywhere there is evidence of technology getting smaller and cheaper, easier to be distributed and embedded. Distinguishing computers as separate objects becomes more and more difficult, as embedded computing shows up everywhere, in toll booths and grocery store check-out lanes, cars' tire-pressure sensors, in automated teller machines—even in toys with internal sensors that can react to human touch and praise.

While technology is everywhere in the built environment—temperature control, air quality monitoring, heating, cooling, security cameras, motion sensors, and powered window blinds—there are limited standards that allow the multiple technologies or systems to work together. Building controls rest in the hands of various business operators, engineers, and facility managers, each of whom has a partial view into the building. Information that could be shared, like drawings and specifications, are frequently outdated, rarely maintained in sync with the building itself. Computation is everywhere, but there remain barriers to its effective use.

As occupants of buildings, we have days when we are too hot, too cold, have too little light or too much glare on our screens. We have no space to meet, no privacy, too much quiet, too much noise. We spend too much time looking for each other. We own too much unused space, burn lights when no one is around to use

AN EVERYWARE WORLD
Adam Greenfield provides a starting point for answering the questions raised by ubiquitous computing in his book *Everyware*, his name for a world replete with smart and connected things. The book is a collection of 80 theses; each is a starting point for an important and needed conversation about how we are changing the world and how it is changing us. In the last section he asks, "How do we safeguard our prerogatives in an everyware world?" How we answer this question will significantly determine how we adapt to the change initiated by smart things.

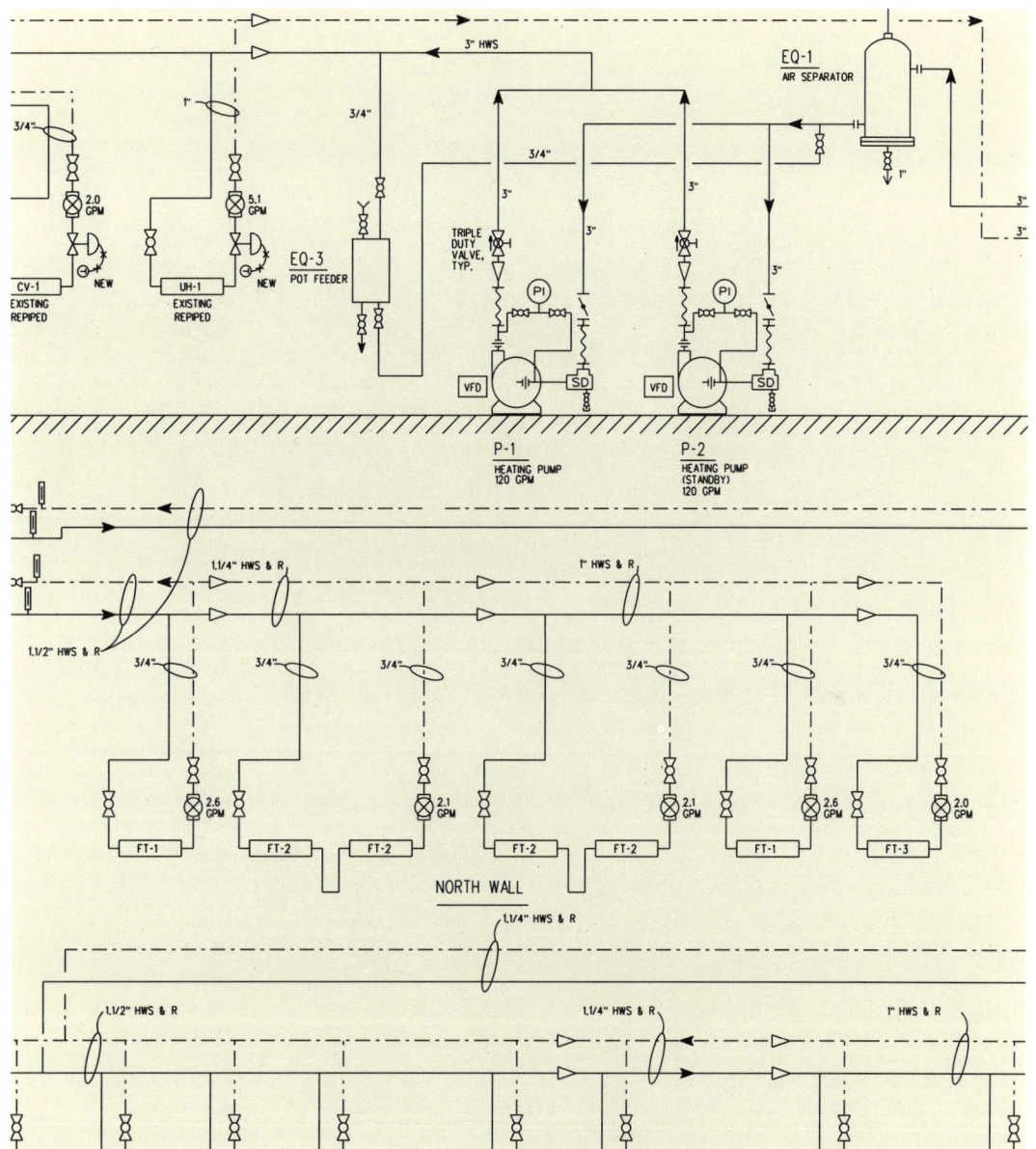

FOCUS ON COMFORT

"Whatever arguments are made concerning the adequacy of our present HVAC designs, they lose strength very quickly when the occupants are consulted. For decades, surveys of building occupants have shown their biggest complaint about their workplace is the lack of a comfortable thermal environment. More recent surveys of office building occupants confirm that this long-standing complaint is unchanging. A recent BOMA survey shows occupants consider the two most important elements in a workspace to be thermal comfort and air quality. The same survey shows that lack of occupant control and lack of adequate comfort constitute the two largest complaints occupants have about their buildings."

–Thomas Hartman, P.E.,
"The 'Comfort Industry':
A 21st Century Opportunity"

them, or start a meeting 10 minutes late, trying to connect to the network, launch the projector, set up the video-conferencing. We lose time and money every day.

As Bill Buxton writes in *Sketching User Experiences*, computing products "will be embedded in buildings that constitute our homes, schools, businesses, and cars. In ways that we are only starting to even imagine, much less understand, they will reshape who does what, where, when, why, how, with whom, for how much, and for how long." Technology will affect the built environment in ways that we can't yet imagine and in ways that may be increasingly important to who we are. Robert Kronenburg, author of *Flexible: Architecture That Responds to Change*, describes the built environment as a "malleable extension of who we are and how we live."

When an environment computes in a way that makes sense to us, we will have properly harnessed its potential power. We can change the way we think about buildings, from design to construction, operation, use, and repurposing. A building that computes can operate more efficiently, create more comfortable spaces, and, most importantly, change to meet changing needs.

Toward connection and meaning

Blogs, MySpace, Facebook, Flicker, YouTube, Twitter, World of Warcraft: The widespread adoption of social technologies shows the value people place on being able to create and share meaning, express themselves, connect with others—known or unknown, stay informed of what's happening among their families or friends or broader communities. The ability to control and shape their digital worlds has also raised people's expectations for influence in the physical world, as evidenced by self-authored ring tones, custom apparel, and self-designed automobile detailing.

What Frances Cairncross termed "the death of distance" as an impact of communications technology might be broadened to "the death of physical place." If your social networks are all online, where are you when you participate in them? If you conduct your business through e-mail, online, and by phone, where is your

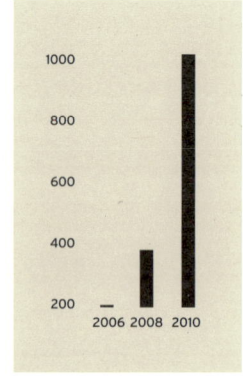

INDIVIDUALS CREATE MEANING
The International Data Corporation (IDC) reports that by 2010 the amount of information in the digital universe will be 988 exabytes. This is about 18 million times all of the information in all of the books ever written. IDC also predicts that 70 percent of this information will be posted by individuals for personal expression and use. This universe will continue to expand at an accelerating rate—with information being created, replicated, shared, and stored.

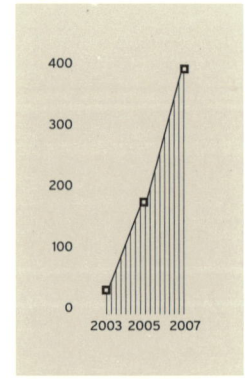

BLOGS ADOPTED QUICKLY
According to Technorati, the number of weblogs has doubled every six months for at least the last four years.

workplace? If you can choose to spend time in digital environments where you're in control of your participation and contribution, or in a physical environment where you feel disconnected and powerless, where will you choose to be?

We don't believe that we're served by leaving the physical environment behind, living in entirely digital communities. People can't communicate completely through text and images. We derive meaning and energy through our presence and the physical company of others, feeding both our work and our play. This may account for the coffee-shop-as-workspace, where members of digital communities share a communal physical space.

The digital world exists within but a completely separate experience from the physical world—aside from power outlets and wireless connection. The question for the future is how we can incorporate aspects of the digital world into the physical environment to provide meaning, connection, and empowerment. The Media Architecture Group shows a beginning, collecting examples from around the world of information technology merging into and changing architecture. Within the group's archives are entire building facades that act as changeable display surfaces, interior rooms in which the walls and ceiling are screens, the eight-story-high kinetic sculpture that is the symbol of the London Stock Exchange, and the Aquatic Center constructed in Beijing, whose exterior walls glow, in a bubble design, with color-changing LED light.

Many of the examples we see use large-scale building elements as canvas or media display; the same technologies can be the basis for expression by and interaction with occupants and passersby. Architecture has always been society's reflection of itself—the community as author. The way in which it does so can change, and is beginning to, both at the individual and community levels.

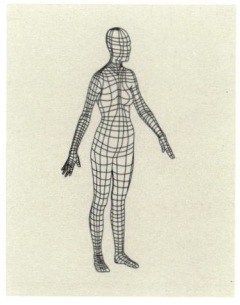

THE DRAW OF THE VIRTUAL WORLD
Edward Castronova, associate professor in the Department of Telecommunications at Indiana University, has written a book called *Exodus To The Virtual World*. He points to the enormous growth in online games and virtual worlds like Second Life and suggests that the ability to 'disappear from reality' could have unexpectedly profound effects on society.

Castronova draws parallels to the 17th century, when thousands of people left Britain for the New World—with effects on new societies in North America but also on the societies left behind. According to BBC News, he says that "while some people will be colonists—'the virtual frontier opens up and off they go and disappear'—others will just use virtual worlds to get together with distant family and friends.... There will be a group of people that spends all their lives there, and the big question is the size of this group."

"We forget how many people there are, and we have to ask ourselves, how exciting is the game of life for most people out there?" Castronova said.

SUSTAINABLE, CHANGEABLE
The Beijing National Aquatic Center, begun in December 2003 for the 2008 Olympics, is both visually compelling and energy efficient. The steel building is covered with a membrane of LED-lit "bubbles." The membrane also absorbs solar radiation, enabling a 30 percent reduction in energy costs.

Toward new economics of place

Retail stores measure the value of space by sales per square foot. Theaters know what percentage of their seats they've filled. In manufacturing, square footage is part of the cost overhead equation; lean principles have allowed use of industrial space to become more and more efficient—frequently surpassing managers' expectations.

But in an economy with knowledge and service as increasingly large parts of our commercial output, we're without metrics for measuring the value of space for knowledge and service workers. Is it workstation occupancy? How, then, factor in community space, the collaboration that happens outside the office, travel to suppliers, research partners, and customers?

It's not surprising, perhaps, that we're without reliable metrics for the value of knowledge worker facilities, when we've yet to agree on measures for the value of knowledge work. How much thinking should a person do in a day? How innovative should that thinking be? When can you quantify the value of an innovation? How do you assign credit for the results of collaboration?

Everyone agrees that organizations need to attract and empower people who do knowledge work. We understand that they will collaborate with colleagues who draw paychecks from different organizations, live in different hemispheres, and may speak different languages. With available technology, they will be mobile in their work and in their leisure. Boundaries between and social expectations of roles, ages, places, time, genders, and work and private lives are all dissolving or moving. These workers will take their expertise, network, and digital file boxes so they can efficiently get to work any place, with a new or old team, or within a new organization.

For the individual, this change can be wonderfully empowering. From a work manager's point of view, the same shifts seem as if the world is falling apart. For a vice president of real estate, it becomes more difficult to decide to build or lease space, how much,

NEW MEASURES NEEDED
Productivity has long been measured by the ratio of input to output. This works in manufacturing or service jobs where the tasks are repetitive and materials are tangible. For people who work primarily with knowledge, how do we value units of information used as inputs? How do we gauge the quality of outputs? If the tasks are different from day to day, how do we track the ratio over time?

and for what expectations of use. Organizations evaluate trade-offs they're unaccustomed to, choosing between investing in mobile technology or in spaces workers may or may not come to.

The future is ambiguous—for the metrics of a knowledge economy and the implications for real estate to support that economy. Designing for change is the best approach for protecting investments as work strategies evolve. This is the era of pliancy: emergent structures, fluid and permeable boundaries, intangible assets, rapid evolution, and a new kind of economics.

Toward a balance of transparency and security

Security, in both political and civic terms, has become a high-profile concern in recent years. We live in a time of increased awareness and expectations for our nation, cities, schools, and neighborhoods to be safe. Parents check on their kids—or pets—in daycare via webcams. They provide teenagers cell phones with GPS so they can check on their whereabouts on the Web. Emergency responders use the same tools to determine the closest vehicle to the accident they've pinpointed and then determine the quickest route to the location.

The industry supporting the culture of security, as well as the technology developments feeding the industry itself, have compounded at an accelerated rate. Wall Street investors have focused their attention on international security companies. Technology advances in this field span sophisticated camera systems, artificial intelligence systems for mining data, face and behavior recognition software, all working to detect patterns in a crowd or in an urban space. According to the Chinese government trade association for surveillance companies, "the Chinese surveillance market will expand to $43.1 billion by 2010, compared with less than $500 million in 2003." It is reported that under the "Safe Cities program adopted by the government last year, 660 cities will be adopting high-tech surveillance systems." In North America, police agencies, jails, fire stations,

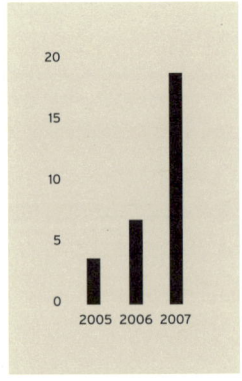

NETWORKING FOR ALL
Facebook has been on track to double in size once every six months, with 100,000 users each day. In spite of its early reputation as a tool for networking college students, the fastest growth is among those 25 and over. More than 60 percent of Facebook users are not college age.

banks, teller machines, airports, train and subway stations, convenience stores, internet cafes, or neighborhood communities are not only everyday spaces, but also customers of an expanding surveillance industry.

Countering this is a culture losing its concern with the specter of "Big Brother," a pervasive new culture of transparency. More and more information is available about people and what they do, think, like, and dislike. Facebook has more than 64 million active users, posting updates to their friends and digital networks, uploading 14 million photos a day. Technorati, a blog search engine, tracked more than 112 million blogs as of December 2007; 1.4 blogs were created every second of every day. News organizations expand their coverage by soliciting viewers' videos of accidents, weather events, and crimes.

It is easy to see the potential, even at an urban scale, of the effects of technology for computing in space, demonstrating, in the urban landscape, a new way of understanding our environments and connectivity within them. In the project Participatory Urbanism, the Intel Research Lab explored how the augmentation of mobile devices with sensors for air quality, noise pollution, and UV levels, could empower citizens to "super-sample" their cities and environments. Data could then be plotted into Google Earth and a new color-coded urban zoning map would appear based on, for example, carbon monoxide levels or air quality. Similar bottom-up approaches are now supporting exploratory data analyses examining urban crime. Initiatives such as oakland. crimespotting.org by Stamen Design, which use police reports of crime plotted on a city map that continuously updates on the Web, or the successful 2007 campaign "The Eyes of New York," which reached out to citizens with a specific call to action – "if you see something, say something" – indicate a shift from a centralized control model to a decentralized and participatory approach to security in our urban environments.

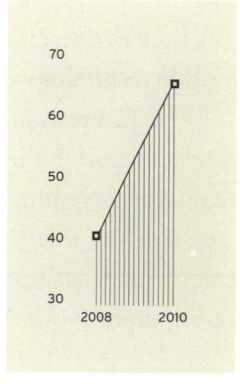

HEAVY INVESTMENT IN SECURITY TECHNOLOGY
According to an IDC (International Data Corporation) white paper sponsored by EMC Corp, "spending on security-specific software is already nearly $40 billion a year; by 2010 it will be $65 billion, or close to 5 percent of total IT spending. Add the software, hardware, and networks needed to support those security products and you are up over 10 percent of IT spending."

EVERYONE EVERYWHERE
"The Eyes of New York" campaign from the Metropolitan Transportation Authority, launched in 2003, engaged the public in security on subways, buses, and commuter rail lines. William A. Morange, head of security for the organization, explained, "It is impossible for the police departments to be everywhere and see everything. Our passengers extend our reach and—by sharing their information—make the system safer."

Ensuring the security of our cities, buildings, and information systems and networks is accepted as a fundamental business consideration for the design of both physical and digital spaces. Buildings judged insecure are already obsolete. Insecure information systems are essentially unusable. We can predict that the convergence of the need for security, new technologies, and changing attitudes about transparency and engagement will lead to new, empowered relationships with our future environments.

These five areas of change intersect to illuminate different ways of thinking about the environment and how it is designed, built, and occupied. They have started us on a path to a sustainable built environment that offers rich experience made possible by digital technologies.

WHAT IF OUR ENVIRONMENTS WERE PROGRAMMABLE?

What if our buildings could give and receive
INFORMATION?
Information like

sound,
scent,
color,
dimension,
line,
pattern,
light,
mass?

movement,
energy use,
occupancy,
temperature,
humidity,
light,
air quality,
voice volume?

Information like

Elvis has left the building.
Monica and Li-Young had a baby girl.

What if information could be used as a design
MATERIAL?

Can the next tenant
choose the color of the room,
by remote control?

Can your presentation
be broadcast by any wall?
Anywhere?

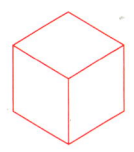

Can a room communicate?

What if our physical

NEIGHBORHOODS

knew us as well as our digital ones do?

What if we could easily share our *digital* lives with our *physical* friends, and vice versa?

What if our buildings let us stay connected?	Would we know when an unknown person has entered the building, the campus, the neighborhood?	Would buildings tell us who's there, and where?	Would we collaborate more easily as we become more familiar to one another?

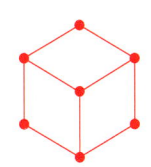

What if we had more
choices and control
in our environments?

Could we design our own personal

EXPERIENCES?

Could Clarice **reprogram** the light fixtures in her shop by herself?

Could Jared **choose** lower light in the morning, brighter light in the afternoon?

Could Ahmed **cool off** his cubicle while Cynthia warms hers?

Could
the marketing team
understand
their energy use
and
work together
to reduce it?

What if buildings never became
OBSOLETE?

Could buildings
be **reprogrammed**,
rather than
renovated?   devalued?   demolished?

Could the same operating system
be used to program either a clinic
or a performing arts center?

What if our buildings grew

SMARTER

the more we used them?

Could buildings

gather historical data to help us understand our environments better?

help us understand what they need to remain healthy and secure?

talk to the system, and the system to the parts, even as they are being constructed?

IF OUR HABITATS WERE PROGRAMMABLE, WHAT WOULD WE ASK OF THEM?

OUR EXPLORATION
OF PROGRAMMABILITY

The Herman Miller Creative Office didn't set out to pursue programmable environments. We recognized the same societal forces as did many of our research colleagues in other organizations. We had some biases and beliefs—specifically, that people and their experiences are important and often don't get the attention they should. That environmental sustainability is, as it's now widely recognized, one of the leading issues for current generations to address on behalf of future generations. That the infusion of technology into every aspect of our lives both is inevitable and offers enormous potential for good. And, of course, given the longstanding focus of Herman Miller's research and innovation, that the built environment is worthy of investment as both a reflection and an enabler of human endeavor.

Our charter was to identify ways to create value for all of the parties involved in built environments—those who build them, maintain them, manage them, furnish them, and use them. We scouted many different areas—innovations in solid state lighting, the interaction of wearable computing with environments, design informatics, DC electrical distribution, indoor air quality, flexible ducts, and environmentally powered sensors. We generally kept these explorations separate. But the more we explored, the more we saw value in the connections between things that are not, in conventional practices, connected. We found possibilities like:

- Using lighting technology and new textile technology as a way to define adaptive space
- Integrating lighting, audio, and display capabilities into space-making elements
- Finding ways to collect building-use data and integrate the data into renovation projects
- Designing single systems for utility delivery—that combine, for example, electricity and communication for control
- Activating ceiling elements, generally simple covers for plenum spaces, to create temporary dedicated-use spaces

EXPERIMENTS IN FORM
The photos on the following six pages document our experimentation in adaptable forms incorporating technology.

This fabric-tube landmark (above) could be easily changed or moved by people nearby. A digital light, also relocated easily, shines directly into the tube from its top.

Because our goal was to create new commercial value, whatever we did needed commercial viability. Finding opportunity in the space between highly specific construction trades and building operations is easy; executing that opportunity commercially is not. All of the trades work in service of building owners and occupants, who share the same measures of neither value nor success.

The owner looks for—among other things—the highest rate of return on investment. Occupants have a range of values, including comfort, security, identity, and productivity. In the squeeze between these two worldviews, it's often the occupant's experience that is sacrificed: In commercial environments today, he can't open a window. He can't find a light switch. Thermostats don't appear to have any effect. He wanders the corridors, hoping that the wayfinding scheme will become clear. Often it doesn't, because the warren has evolved since the design was installed, and there is no clarity to find.

Exploring the possibilities in the intersections led us to believe that it was possible—because of converging capabilities and sensibilities—to resolve the tension between two competing objectives:

1. *Enable people who use buildings to be active agents in the creation and evolution of the spaces that support their activities*

2. *Preserve or improve the economic equation for people who build and own buildings*

And we believed that these simultaneous benefits would be accompanied by a third:

3. *Lessen the environmental impact of the built environment— from construction through continuous reuse*

Because the experience of space we envisioned was so important to the concept, we built a lab and modeled some of our ideas. We had free rein in exploration at this point, focused by three criteria: increase flexibility, increase sustainability, and hold or reduce costs.

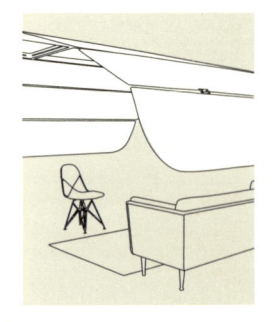

CEILINGS
We experimented with articulating ceilings that enclosed a space from the top and included video display screens. In another approach, baffles diffused light and shaped the space.

Documentation of work in progress

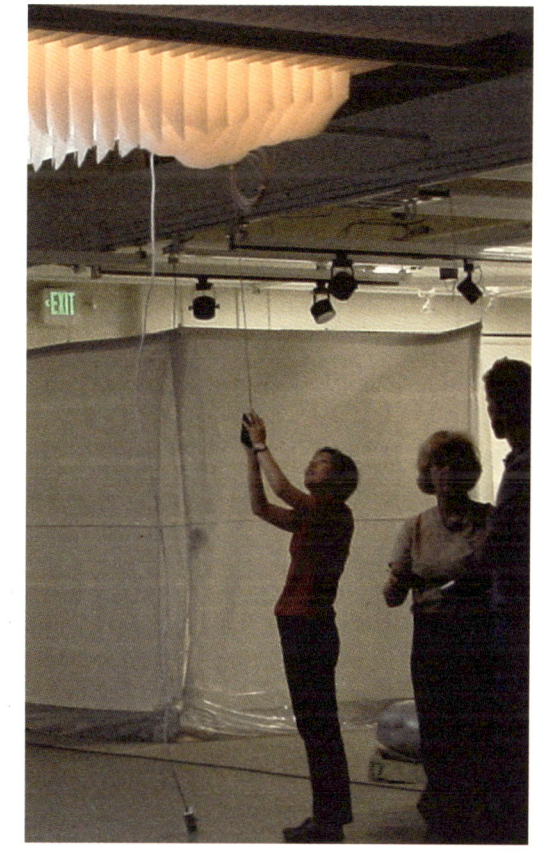

OUR EXPLORATION 53

Realizing that space planning is normally done from the floor up, we asked what would happen if you worked from the top down. We built variations on articulating ceilings that could define space, even contain videoconferencing. We saw that planning from the top down let you use gravity instead of fighting gravity—leading to lighter-weight materials for dividing space. We used light to create the effect of ceilings and walls. We replaced spot lighting with fully illuminated LED planes. We saw that the hodgepodge of ductwork, cabling, and wiring that finds its way into the ceiling is part of the rigidity we now accept in buildings.

We experimented extensively with new technology. We set up a PC in the lobby and made ID cards. When you entered the space, you provided the PC with information about your preferences in music, air, and light, and then swiped the ID card. As you moved through the lab, these inputs caused changes in light levels and colors, temperature, and sounds. We used LED lighting for wayfinding, including using light arrows to create pathways on the floor to help people find books in a library.

We looked for ways that people could reconfigure space with no construction skills and no more than a stepladder—changing a space from library carrels to a conference room in 10 or 15 minutes. We prototyped textile walls that could be moved manually or mechanically to change a space from a lobby to a meeting room to a corridor.

These experiments in temporal spaces led us to think about decision-making during the design and construction process. What if the last responsible moment to make decisions could be moved later in the game, much closer to the actual use of a building? And what if more decisions could be reserved for users of a building—because who knows better what an environment needs to do at each moment?

Through all of our experimentation, we checked back against our objectives, accounting for each stakeholder, from the building owner to the user. We defined the benefit to each and verified that

ROOMS
We looked for ways to create temporary rooms with lightweight materials that could be moved easily into place by people who need a place to meet. Light and pattern gave the walls more visual substance.

Documentation of work in progress

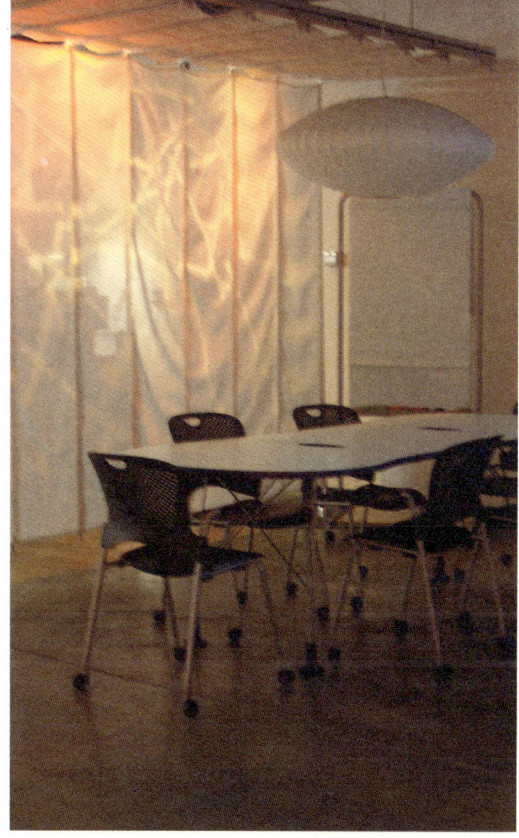

OUR EXPLORATION 55

the net effect was more flexibility and sustainability. We learned much that set the stage for further development:

- People need to interact as directly as possible with the environment, not with a facsimile of the environment or other intermediary. The easier it is to change, the less people postpone change.
- Conventional utility provision is a critical obstacle to more flexibility in environments.
- While modularity has been well explored to achieve flexibility in physical space, programmability has not.
- Placemaking components that are lightweight and easy to move don't benefit just the people who can use them, they also require fewer resources than conventional construction.
- Environments can have both physical and digital dimensions—like much in the rest of our lives.
- Everyone benefits from delaying the last responsible moment for space-design decision-making as long as possible.

Having gotten this far in describing our vision, we focused on developing a platform for programmability, one that would bring flexibility to utilities that currently constrain adaptability and provide a network for communication and data gathering throughout an environment.

WALLS
Walls made of textiles and other lightweight materials were movable and able to be re-skinned for display in, for example, a retail environment.

Documentation of work in progress

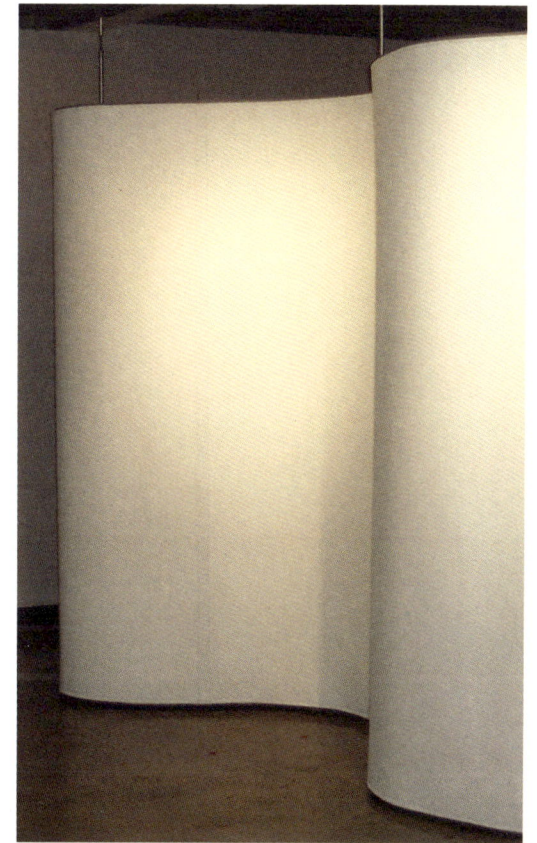

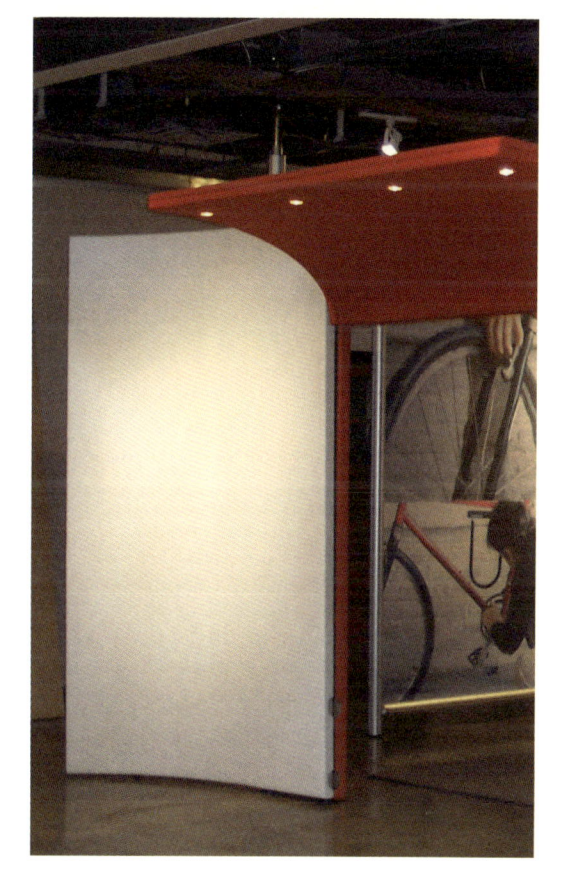

OUR EXPLORATION 57

ADAPTABLE CONFERENCE ROOM
One large room can be changed in minutes into two, each with its own scene settings for multiple uses.

DIGITAL CONTROLS
When they're digital, controls can be easily associated or reassociated with specific fixtures, without rewiring.

OCCUPANT COMFORT
Underfloor air handling and diffuser controls facilitate fine-tuning by users of air flow and temperature.

A PLATFORM TO BUILD ON

The infrastructure developed with the future vision of a programmable environment in mind became Convia, first available from Herman Miller in 2007. Convia is designed for inclusiveness and integration: Its platform supports multiple widely used protocols to enable evolution to keep pace with our learning. All of the components and capabilities for the programmable environment must evolve in the same way that environments will adapt—with use, with change, in community with the people who build, manage, and inhabit buildings.

TRADITIONAL INCREMENTAL/DISPARATE SYSTEMS

ENERGY MANAGEMENT
+
AUDIO VISUAL CONTROL
+
LIGHTING CONTROL
+
ELECTRICAL INFRASTRUCTURE

CONVIA INTEGRATED SYSTEMS

REPORTING / LIGHTING CONTROL / AUDIO VISUAL SYSTEM / ENERGY CONTROL / DIGITAL CONTROLLED ELECTRICAL PLATFORM

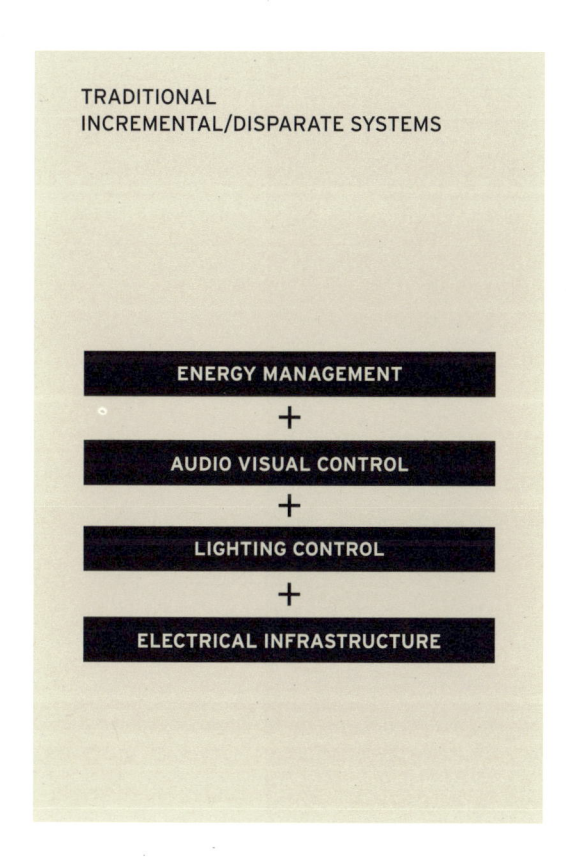

AN INTEGRATED APPROACH
As a platform for the programmable environment, the Convia system enables a flexible and integrated approach to both utility delivery and control.

An intelligent power delivery platform, integrating a communication network with a modular electrical system, provides the foundation to build upon. Microcontrollers distribute intelligence throughout the electrical infrastructure, creating a network of power nodes and zones that can be programmed to respond to changing needs in the environment. Lighting controls, instead of being embedded in the existing electrical infrastructure, are separate from the power delivery system and thus able to be easily changed. Components connected to the Convia system are able to communicate with any other component connected to the system.

The power delivery platform has cost-reduction and environmental benefits. As a modular system, it can be installed in less time than conventional utility wiring, with better coordination among construction trades and fewer change orders during the project. When installed, it sets the stage for effective energy management—and adapting as energy requirements change. When a larger-scale change is needed, the electrical infrastructure can be reconfigured quickly and easily; all components can be reused. This not only reduces the cost of change, it eliminates dumpsters filled with conventional but no longer appropriate wires and cables.

People can control objects in a Convia environment through two interfaces. The first is the simplest: a handheld, wireless, two-button wand. You can use it to link any light or receptacle or a series of them, with any sensor or switch. Aim the wand at a light, and then at a switch, and the association is made instantly. Aim the wand at a second light, and that switch will also operate that light. This level of simplicity enables people to participate in changing their environments.

INDIVIDUAL COMFORT
Art, a creative director for a global news magazine, works long days and nights. He doesn't want to waste his time fiddling for comfort and has programmed his office to shift from day to night by setting scenes. (1) By day he hosts a constant stream of intense, stand-up meetings with editors, photographers, and designers, poring over work and proofs. By night, he works at his desk, catching up on correspondence and preparing for the next day's meetings. (2) Blinds are drawn by day to control light color and intensity, but open at night for the view. (3) His glass wall is opaque by day for privacy and transparent at night. (4) He keeps the office cool when people will share his space and warmer when he's alone.

OUR EXPLORATION 61

The second interface is through application management software on a personal computer. While easy to use, this software allows all protocols and subsystems to interoperate, providing both a holistic view of the building and one point of interaction with multiple systems or applications. The software can reflect a hierarchy of access and control: A building manager operates at the building-wide scale (setting the coolest and warmest air temperatures, for example), while individuals affect the areas of the building that they use (adjusting for comfort within the range).

Both the adaptability of the design and the ease of change through simple interfaces enable inhabitants to act as co-designers. Beyond those factors, one of the most important enablers of the continuous evolution of a rich experience is information—information that tells us what's working and what's not, information that indicates possibilities.

Information is at work before anyone enters a building, because the HVAC system operation can be based on data of past needs, not on someone's arbitrary or well-intentioned decision. Information continues to play a role throughout the day, provided by individuals about their preferences and provided to the people in the building; reporting gives immediate, actionable feedback on energy use, space utilization, and more.

In the programmable environment and with the Convia platform, any event or action can be tracked and stored—with information from multiple sources and different application types within the environment. That data can be reported on in standard ways, but also queried for new insights. The Convia knowledge development platform is designed to adapt to organizations' needs, but also so that we can learn from many experiences what it means when an environment shares information with itself and with its managers and inhabitants. What we're looking for is continuous evolution on a perpetually larger scale.

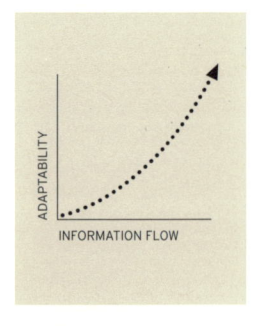

INFORMATION FEEDS ADAPTABILITY
Feedback to occupants and building managers enables adaptation to happen more quickly and more effectively.

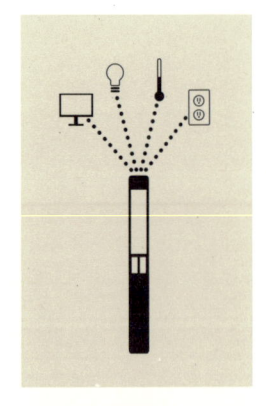

INTUITIVE INTERFACE
The Convia wand was designed to be simple and intuitive and to give the user the most direct possible control over the environment.

TOOLS FOR THE PROGRAMMABLE DESIGN MEDIUM

We believe these components, reflected in the Convia platform, are required to create a programmable environment:

- A communication network for things
- Easy connectivity for things to the network
- Simple communication by people with things
- Intuitive rules for interacting with the space
- Immediacy of results
- Means to link interdependent devices and save preferred settings for "scene control"
- "Edit Undo" recovery from mistakes
- Storage for data from the environment
- Analysis tools to understand the data
- A standard structural interface that is part of the architecture and infrastructure of the interior space
- Simple mechanical attachment for physical objects to the structural interface, requiring only common hand tools

The parts of the Convia environment are connected—nodes on a network—and they are all providers and receivers of information as well as physical objects. You can configure and reconfigure the relationships between controlling and controlled components and building subsystems and provide rudimentary brains—in the form of sensors—to any component you would like to include as a node on your network. Sensors can respond to many kinds of input—light, motion, force, chemistry—to operate or report on one or a series of components. The sun rising and shining through a window can turn lights off and adjust the heat. A motion-detecting sensor can turn lights on, run a wall display, issue ambient sound or scent, trigger a fountain, report on room occupancy, or chair occupancy, or perform all of these in the morning and a different series in the afternoon. Once components are part of the network, you can define and store associations between them.

And any node on the network also provides information about how often it's used, what commands it has executed, and other factors so that the whole environment, the building zones, and scenes themselves can continuously evolve.

FIRST FINDINGS ON ENERGY SAVINGS

A study conducted by The Weidt Group, an independent engineering consultant for high performance buildings, found that offices using the Convia system can gain up to 30 percent in annual energy savings as compared to the ASHRAE standard 90.1-2004, the current energy benchmark for buildings.

Communities throughout the state of California have implemented stringent building codes to meet energy guidelines issued by the California Energy Commission. Southern California Edison is one of the largest electric utilities in the United States and an early adopter of the Convia infrastructure, a technology they are installing in an existing office building, testing an "office of the future" concept.

CONVIA
A HERMAN MILLER COMPANY

MORE ABOUT THE CONVIA PLATFORM

For more information about the Convia infrastructure and how it can contribute to LEED certification, go to www.HMConvia.com.

A platform in use

As a foundation, Convia demonstrates the potential of programmability and enables us to learn what living consciously with digital and physical aspects of environments offers that we haven't yet considered. Convia is in use at the group's headquarters, outside Chicago, where the inhabitants are full participants. This is how, given development to date, the capabilities play out throughout the day:

When the first employee arrives at the office the alarm system recognizes her and deactivates. Each employee arrives and is welcomed according to preferences:

> Jackie's monitor comes on, and lights overhead come on half-way. The lights will come to full power later in the day, when Jackie needs help to stay alert.

> Matt heads into the break room; the lights come on in response to a sensor. (The sensor has been moved a few times, because at first it triggered when people went by but not into the room.) He grabs a cup of coffee, which is already brewed, and heads to his workstation. Matt is sensitive to computer-screen glare: As he sits down, the adjacent shades lower and the overhead lights stay off.

> Randy's office lights turn on full, his digital frame displays pictures from his European vacation, and the Rolling Stones kick in on the sound system. Because the sunrise is especially bright, the shades lower; usually, Randy enjoys the sun.

> The first thing on Jane's agenda is conducting a webinar. In the conference room, she pushes the button for the webinar "scene"—one of a number of preset combinations of room features. The technology powers up, the shades lower, and the digital LCD screen displays the presentation. John rushes in, claiming he needs the conference room. Short on time before the webinar, Jane chooses not to argue, but to push the button for the room to

PRESSURE FROM STATIC ENVIRONMENT

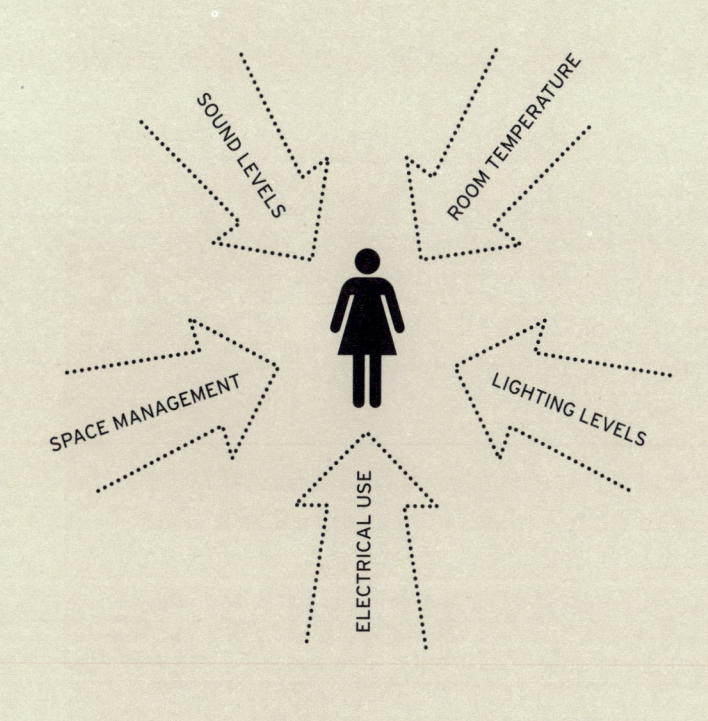

SOUND LEVELS
ROOM TEMPERATURE
SPACE MANAGEMENT
LIGHTING LEVELS
ELECTRICAL USE

HARMONY WITH PROGRAMMABLE ENVIRONMENT

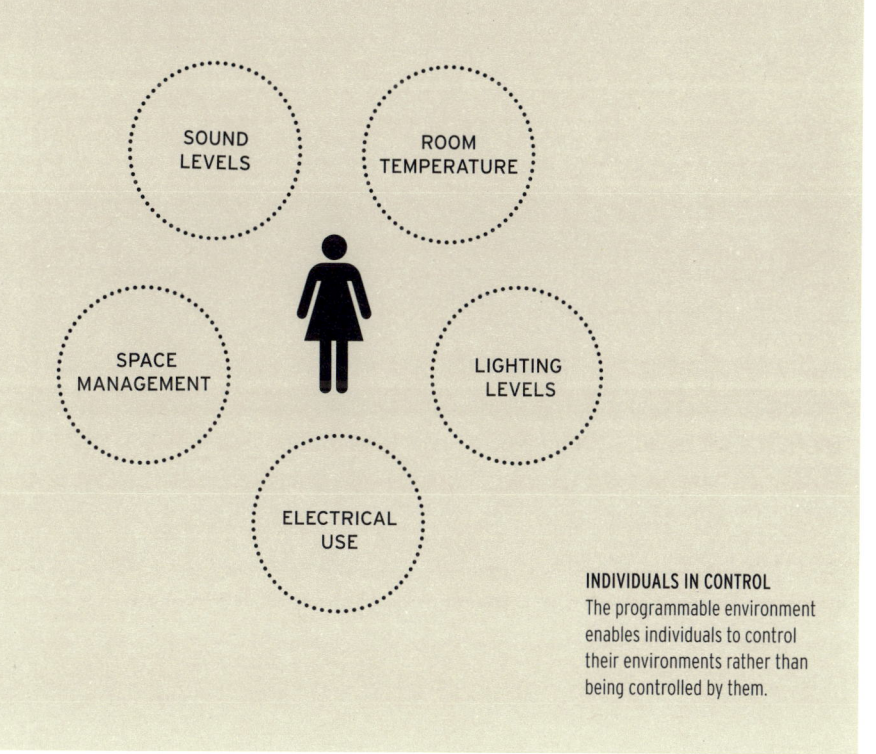

SOUND LEVELS
ROOM TEMPERATURE
SPACE MANAGEMENT
LIGHTING LEVELS
ELECTRICAL USE

INDIVIDUALS IN CONTROL
The programmable environment enables individuals to control their environments rather than being controlled by them.

become two instead of one. The automated wall partitions move into place, the light switches respond accordingly, and the HVAC system creates two zones instead of one.

At lunchtime, the café lights and music come on, encouraging the team to gather to socialize, relax, and set the stage for the afternoon's collaboration. Jane heads out for a run, knowing that she can adjust the HVAC in her workstation for an hour or so afterward while she cools down.

Throughout the day, the ambient light adjusts in response to natural sunlight in the space; public areas like restrooms are lighted only when occupied. Convia reporting shows that the energy use is at or below ASHRAE 2004 codes 90 percent of the time, an improvement over last quarter's 85 percent. The team is invested in this performance, because they can get ongoing information about their performance to energy goals and immediate feedback about what's working and what's not.

The day winds down. The team member who thinks he's last out of the building hits the shut-down "scene" button at the front door, intending to shut down lighting and electrical loads and activate the alarm system. Fortunately, the occupancy sensor in Scott's workstation overrides the building-wide shut-down, because the quiet programmer is still at work.

It is easy to argue that people will prefer environments that make them more comfortable. The Convia platform was designed to give people control over their environments and the tools to redesign and program environments to suit their needs for adaptability, comfort, and convenience. And environments built on a programmable infrastructure will be more valuable to builders and owners—vastly reducing the cost and waste of construction, remodeling, operation, and obsolescence.

VARIETY OF USE
For Angie, a real estate developer, time is money. For every minute a space in one of her buildings sits unoccupied, revenue drops. Programmability has helped her boost profits by letting her change in a day what used to take weeks of planning and construction, even in some of the older buildings she owns downtown. Here Angie works with her tenants to prepare the same space for two very different uses - first a city community college, then a health clinic. Using a stepladder and simple hand tools, she can (1) change out the lights and program special display equipment, (2) reposition occupancy sensors to help tenants understand their use of space, and (3) establish user-defined rules for securing the space.

OUR EXPLORATION 67

ACHIEVING THE PROMISE
OF PROGRAMMABILITY

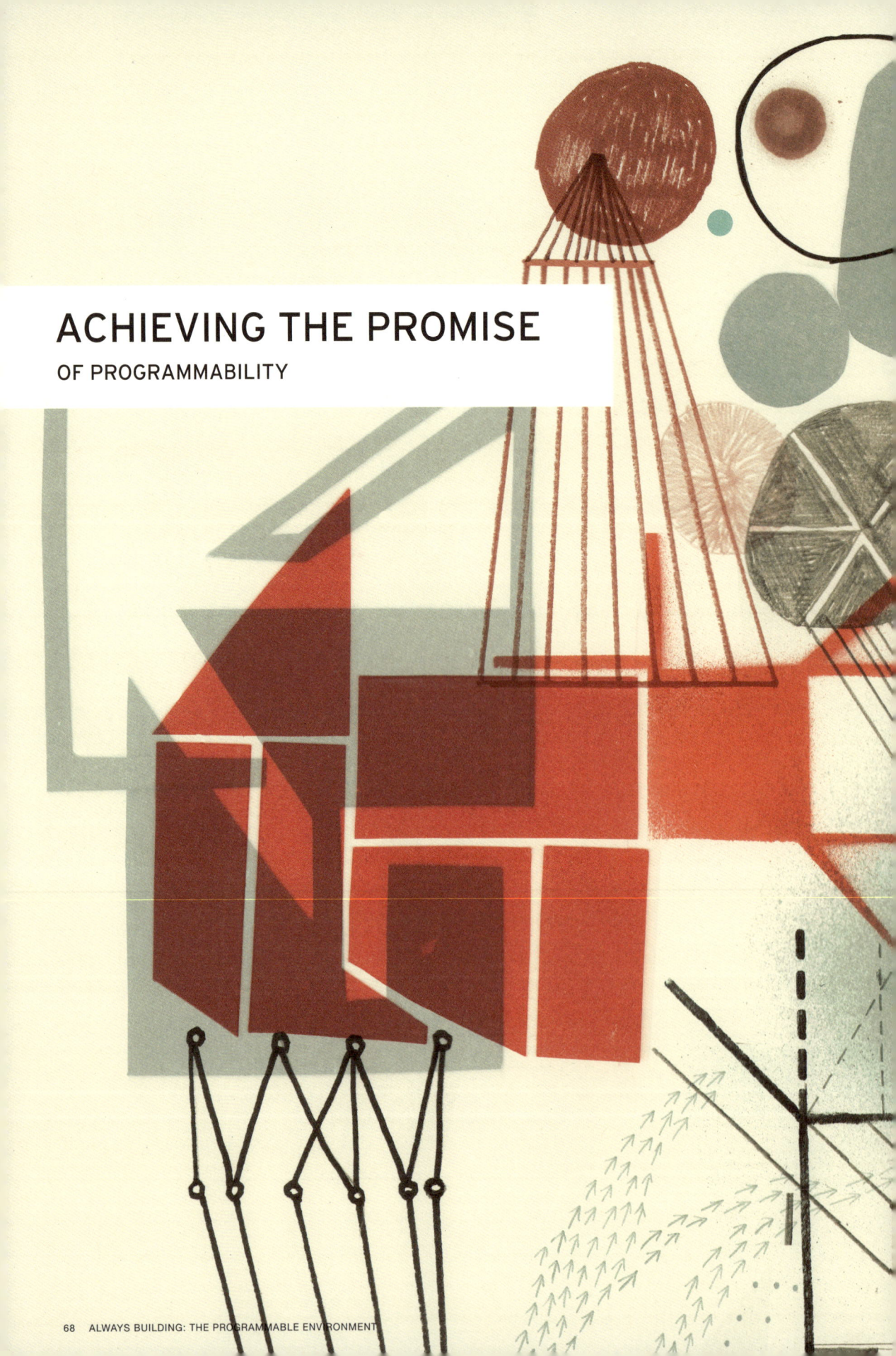

Programmability offers a radical reinvention, a new design medium with a new result. Instead of a building, complete and fixed in time, subject to renovation or demolition when its purpose is no longer relevant, the result is a system designed to evolve in interaction with the people who use the building. A programmable environment redraws the boundaries of architecture, interior design, and facility management. As a new medium, programmability requires new practices, a merging of experience design, interior design, architecture, system design, and engineering. And the always-building environment, as opposed to the built environment, embraces users of the building as co-designers of the space.

To achieve programmable environments, we think about a digital as well as a physical dimension of space. The digital dimension provides a common language for objects within the space to communicate with each other, for people to communicate with objects, for a certain level of security between objects. It provides the means for data to be collected from objects in the space, and for objects to be told how to behave.

The digital dimension means that we think about the physical dimension differently. Instead of having a monolithic electrical system, for example, we need to think about how an electrical system can become modular, simple, and integrated with other systems. Each light fixture can become a node on the network that the building becomes. Instead of a chair being only a chair, a chair can carry a sensor and become another node on the network, providing information about whether and how a space is used.

PEOPLE

PROGRAMMABLE
ENVIRONMENT

DIGITAL
PROPERTIES

PHYSICAL
PROPERTIES

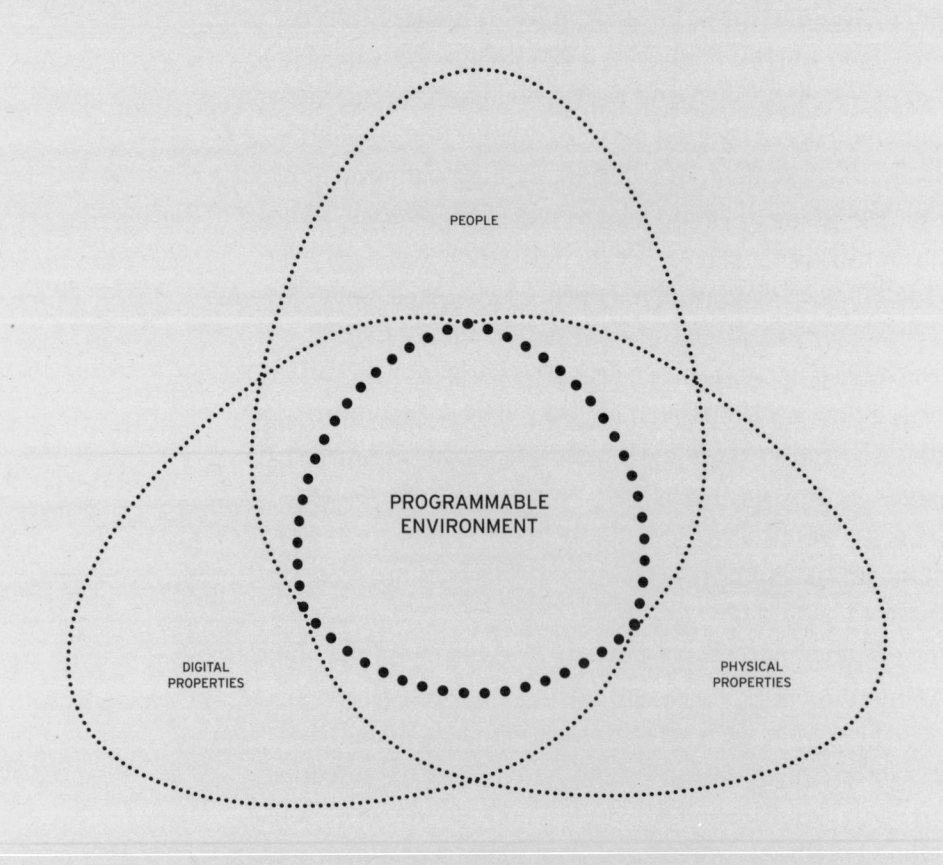

**CONTROL IN DIGITAL AND
PHYSICAL DIMENSIONS**
Programmable environments
give people control over
physical and digital properties.

CREATING THE PROGRAMMABLE ENVIRONMENT

Every design project, whether new construction, renovation, or redesign of an existing space, has unique goals and priorities. For a nonprofit hospital, the highest priority might be the quality of patient care. For a corporate headquarters, trade-offs may be made for optimal presentation of brand attributes. For a call center, perhaps process efficiency, minimizing turnover, or cost-effective operation is the highest priority. Programmability allows—in fact, requires—the design team to think beyond the current explicit program requirements to design on a larger canvas: the next use of the environment and then the use beyond that. Instead of designing a static product that is complete in one moment and becoming obsolete the next, the designer is creating a system that will continuously evolve.

Four principles specific to the programmable environment, interrelated and interdependent, are the basis for achieving this greater impact:

> Maximizing the capacity for adaptation is the focus of programmable design.
>
> The time to effect change is ideally zero.
>
> Design is collaborative and includes people who inhabit a space as co-designers.
>
> Everything is recognized as both physical and digital.

Let's look at each of these principles in detail.

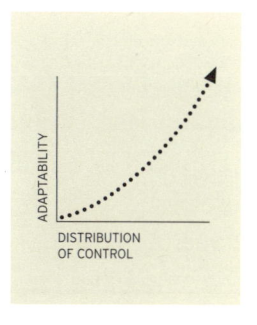

SHARING CONTROL SPEEDS ADAPTATION
Widely distributed control enhances the degree and speed of adaptability, one of the benefits of engaging occupants in interacting with the environment.

Maximizing the capacity for adaption

Among the questions in a building design project is: What is the appropriate distribution of light fixtures in the space? The answer is reached by considering variables including the anticipated use of the space, the illumination requirements for that use, the dimensions of the space, the number and placement of windows, the concept for the experience of the space, and so on. Without reasonable estimates for these variables, an architect or lighting designer won't know what kind of lighting solution to provide.

If the designer is concerned first with adaptability, the design question changes: What kind of lighting system will meet the requirements of potential different uses over the life of the building? Some of the variables are the same, but others change, and the estimates become less certain. A viable design solution is a system that allows for easy change in some key elements: location of fixtures, illumination level, control strategy, and controls locations. Such systems are combinations of modularity and programmability. How control is distributed is the key feature of these systems and critical to adaptability. The axiom is: The more widely distributed the control, the more adaptable the environment.

Control encompasses both authority to act and the locale and scope of the effect; these are social or political determinations. For maximum adaptability, the environment should place as little constraint as possible on how control is distributed, and constraints should be genuine. A simple example is the sprinklers that are part of fire-safety systems. Sprinkler heads are typically hard-plumbed, so relocation is expensive. Sprinkler heads with flexible stainless-steel hoses are now available and offer simpler installation and some, though limited, ability to relocate. In many locales, however, moving a sprinkler head requires an inspection by a fire marshal or other building inspector, which means that the authority to relocate sprinkler heads cannot be distributed to the occupants of a space. Even though occupants cannot make the change, the ability to relocate makes change easier even for licensed trades or professionals.

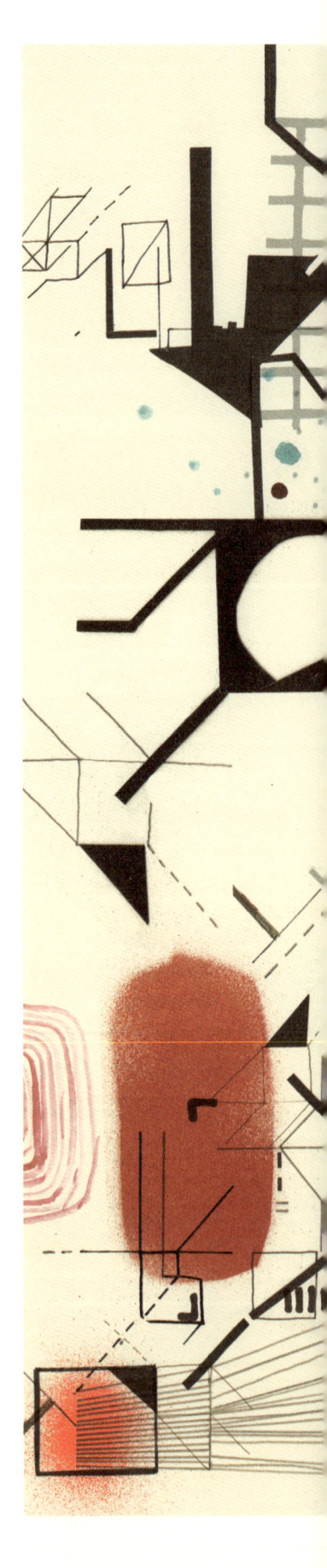

ACHIEVING THE PROMISE 73

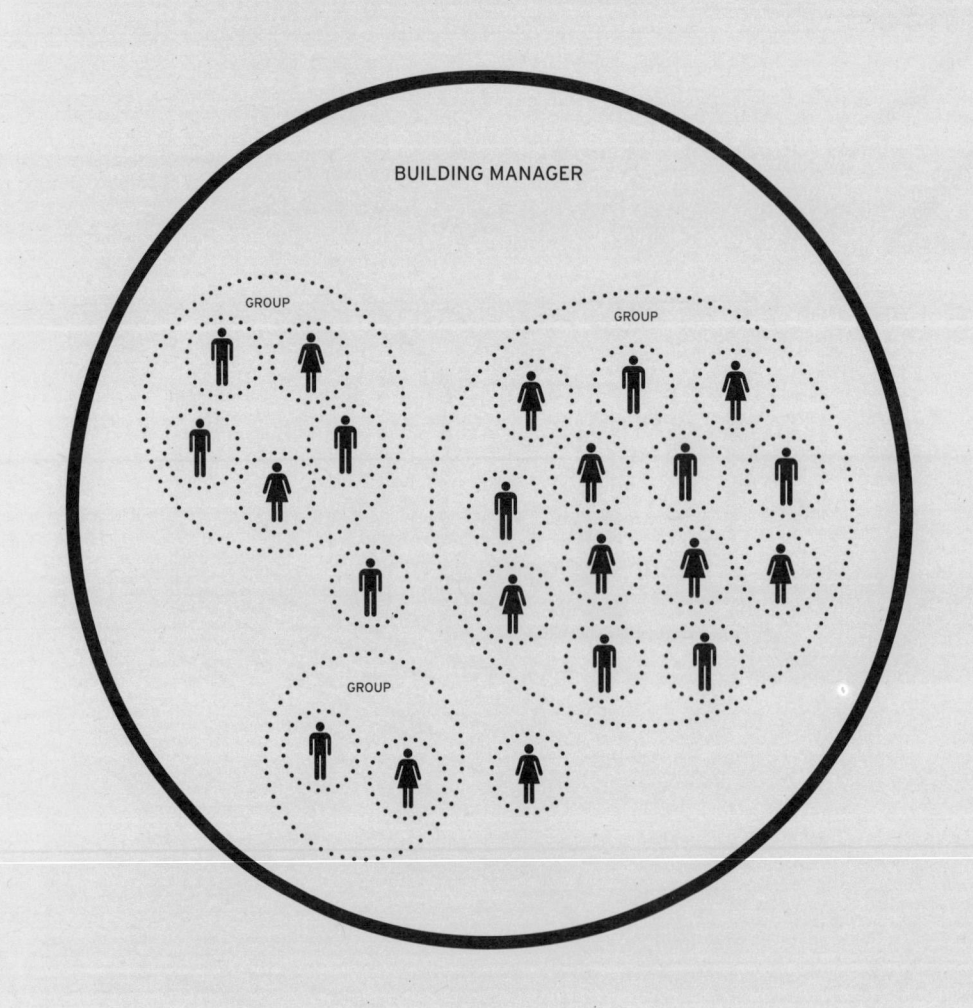

CONTROL AT DIFFERENT LEVELS
A hierarchy of access and control allows the building manager to operate at the building-wide scale, while groups and individuals affect the areas they use.

74 ALWAYS BUILDING: THE PROGRAMMABLE ENVIRONMENT

Interacting with environments will always be governed by rules, whether established by regulation, safety considerations, social norms, or cultures of organizations. Programmable environments don't change that fact, but they will change the rules.

Three simple rules serve as the starting point for designing the social and technical system of the programmable environment:

> The control given to people using the environment today will not limit the interests of the people using the environment in the future.

> The design and implementation of the system enables a hierarchy of priorities and constraints. (For example, a person can change the temperature of his office, but not above 72 degrees.)

> The tools provided to interact with the space are simple and intuitive.

Incorporating adaptability into an environment requires revisiting some long-held notions about space. Boundaries, entryways, and passageways assumed to be permanent will need to be considered in new ways to enable future adaptability. Instead of conventional private areas, we may consider lightweight, easily movable structures for temporary and semi-permanent space division. Finally, new rules governing the actions of all who engage in design and change activities must be conceived and communicated.

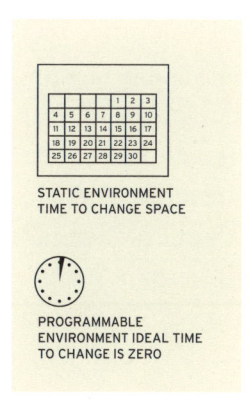

STATIC ENVIRONMENT TIME TO CHANGE SPACE

PROGRAMMABLE ENVIRONMENT IDEAL TIME TO CHANGE IS ZERO

DESIGNED FOR CHANGE
When a facility is designed to change, the time investment required is minimal.

Pursuing zero-time change

The ability of a programmable environment to respond quickly—sometimes immediately—to the desired next state is critical to its ability to adapt. The longer it takes for a change to be made, the more it's postponed by the person who needs it. The longer it's put off, the more people adapt to the inconvenience of the current state, and the further out of touch with the need the current state becomes.

If we plan for instant change, where do we build walls? Where do we place light fixtures and switches, diffusers and ducts? When the design and its use are inseparable, the environment becomes an improvisational production, one in which the elements of the space itself join the people as actors responding to the next cue. Performance in real time is the measure of success.

If the environment can respond immediately—and simply—to a change in needs, the people using the space, and even the people designing the space, can experiment in real time in the space itself. The changes that work will last. Changes that don't work can be quickly undone and something else tried.

The ability to implement change quickly implies, finally, that decisions in the construction process can be made at the last possible moment—keeping options open until we have the most or most current information. We see potential for eliminating waste and inefficiency—and associated environmental impact—in the construction process. Integrating digital technology into building materials, the availability of modular building components, and improvements in design informatics all imply a construction process that is more like a continuous flow (like lean manufacturing) of building material into the form of a building, rather than the staging of materials processed by batch into a structure.

ACHIEVING THE PROMISE

People who inhabit a space are its co-designers

We've introduced the idea that the programmable environment is a design medium. For that to be meaningful, people who inhabit and use a space need to participate in design activities. Robert Kronenburg, who has written often on mobile and portable architecture, elaborates on this idea:

> Flexible architecture requires an attitude to design that integrates the requirements of the present with the possibility to adapt to changing situations in the future.... It is about allowing future users and designers, who will know their own situation best, the leeway to make appropriate decisions when they are needed. This can take the form of spaces and elements that are easily manipulated and altered on a day-to-day basis, or the capacity to be changed fundamentally with minimal disruption and expense as circumstances develop over a longer period. This does not mean that architects now need to focus on designing loose-fitting, non-dedicated environments without character. Instead the ambition should be to create buildings that have integrated, carefully devised systems that are capable of responding to new and varied situations. This is architecture that needs designers' skills more than ever, not to create a product that is perfect on delivery (but is destined for compromise in the future) but one that is capable of taking advantage of other contributors to the building's operation (most importantly the users) during its future lifetime.

The programmable environment is an expression of this attitude. Kronenburg makes clear the need for full and ongoing collaboration between designers and building users throughout

ACHIEVING THE PROMISE 79

the life of the building. Their responsibility—together, as designers and users—is to satisfy current needs and to maintain a design medium that will adapt over time to changing needs of both the organization and the inhabitants of the environment. Such a collaboration is so critical that we consider users to be co-designers— not trained in design, but full participants in design activities.

Programmable environments invite the inhabitant into the control dialog of the building. Simple-to-use interfaces and simple rules for change are prerequisite for user participation. Co-designers must have the freedom to explore and the security to correct mistakes. Providing this invitation to users is a significant challenge to designers. The wand developed for Convia, with its simple rules for associating smart things, is one expression of meeting the challenge.

The first goal of collaborative design activities is always the adaptation of a space to its current purpose. A broader and no less important goal is ensuring future participation of unknown designers and co-designers whose purposes are also unknown. Nature provides the clues for meeting the second goal—variety.

As experiences are more varied and rich, people using the space will be more engaged, and more information will be exchanged on multiple dimensions: What's happening in a workstation, a team, a floor, an entire building? Information teaches people quickly what works and what doesn't, enabling faster adaptation on a perpetually larger scale. Programmable environments provide opportunities for creating variety, and an intelligent infrastructure is part of making this possible.

PROGRAMMABLE
ENVIRONMENT

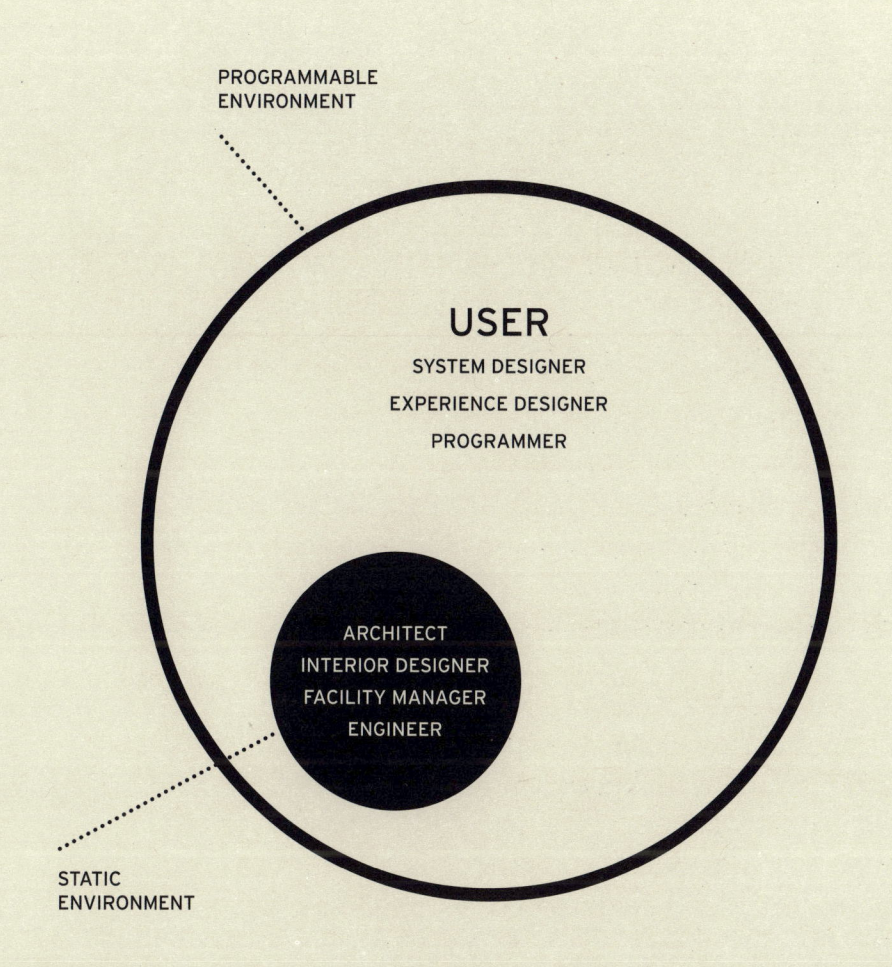

USER
SYSTEM DESIGNER
EXPERIENCE DESIGNER
PROGRAMMER

ARCHITECT
INTERIOR DESIGNER
FACILITY MANAGER
ENGINEER

STATIC
ENVIRONMENT

A DIVERSE DESIGN TEAM
Creating a programmable environment requires a more diverse cross-functional design team, which includes the user as a co-designer.

Recognize everything as both physical and digital

What does it mean when something has digital properties as well as its physical properties? And what do we have to do differently as a result? Photo-sensor-based dimming control provides one example. These systems sense the level of illumination in a space and adjust it to a predetermined level. Their benefits are well documented: energy savings, longer calendar life for lamps, and user comfort. Despite these benefits and almost 20 years on the market, they are used in less than 5 percent of commercial buildings. Barriers to their adoption include purchase cost, a lack of evidence of reliability and cost-effectiveness, system complexity, and the need for the system to be integrated into the building design. Lack of understanding of digital properties plays a role in each of these barriers, but in particular in the last two.

Part of the complexity of systems like that one is that being digital means the potential to be interconnected; while the benefits are generally acknowledged, connectivity increases complexity and requires thoughtful integration. The role of window blinds in lighting control illustrates this interconnectedness. Blinds block daylight to reduce glare or excess direct light. When blinds are closed, more energy is needed for electric illumination. But sometimes blinds are left closed simply because no one opens them—clearly diminishing the energy-savings effectiveness intended for the system.

Recognizing the digital properties of each element and thinking through the implications of connectivity would lead to a system in which the blinds, lights, and light sensors communicated with one another (an example of what is now known as physical computing). This is simple for one window, but at the scale of a commercial building, the complexity is magnified. The digital properties are the same, regardless of the scale; the problem is not with the property but with our ability to use it properly.

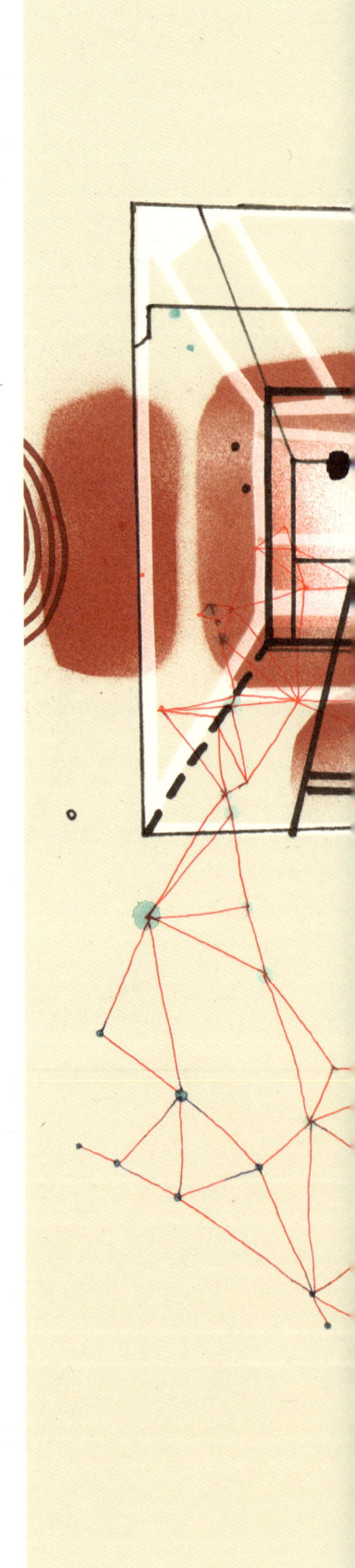

ACHIEVING THE PROMISE 83

Being digital also means having a presence beyond physicality. Drawings, blueprints, records of use, instructions for use, warranties, and user reviews are easily accessible parts of things. All of this data and information can either increase or reduce complexity—depending on how well we understand and use it.

Complex and complicated systems are problematic for users only when the complexity or complication is visible. The dimming control for lighting becomes an acute problem when the user who needs higher illumination can't figure out how to get it. A programmable environment needs to provide the occupant a simple interface—as intuitive as a screwdriver or a hammer— to the digital properties of physical things.

As more and more things are built with digital properties, tools that manipulate those properties become critical. This is especially true in buildings where the expertise of the occupants—and future occupants—cannot be anticipated. In a programmable environment, digital character becomes as important a design consideration as the physicality of an object or the space.

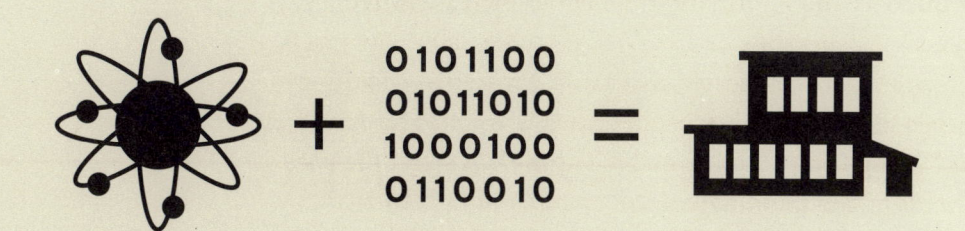

PHYSICAL + DIGITAL = PROGRAMMABLE ENVIRONMENT

STATIC ENVIRONMENT
DISCONNECT BETWEEN ENVIRONMENT AND USER NEEDS

••••••••••••
THE USERS' NEEDS
IN A SPACE

──────────
RESPONSE OF SPACE
TO THE USERS' NEEDS

1 YEAR   3 YEARS   6 YEARS   9 YEARS   12 YEARS   15 YEARS

PROGRAMMABLE ENVIRONMENT
KEEPING PACE WITH CHANGING NEEDS

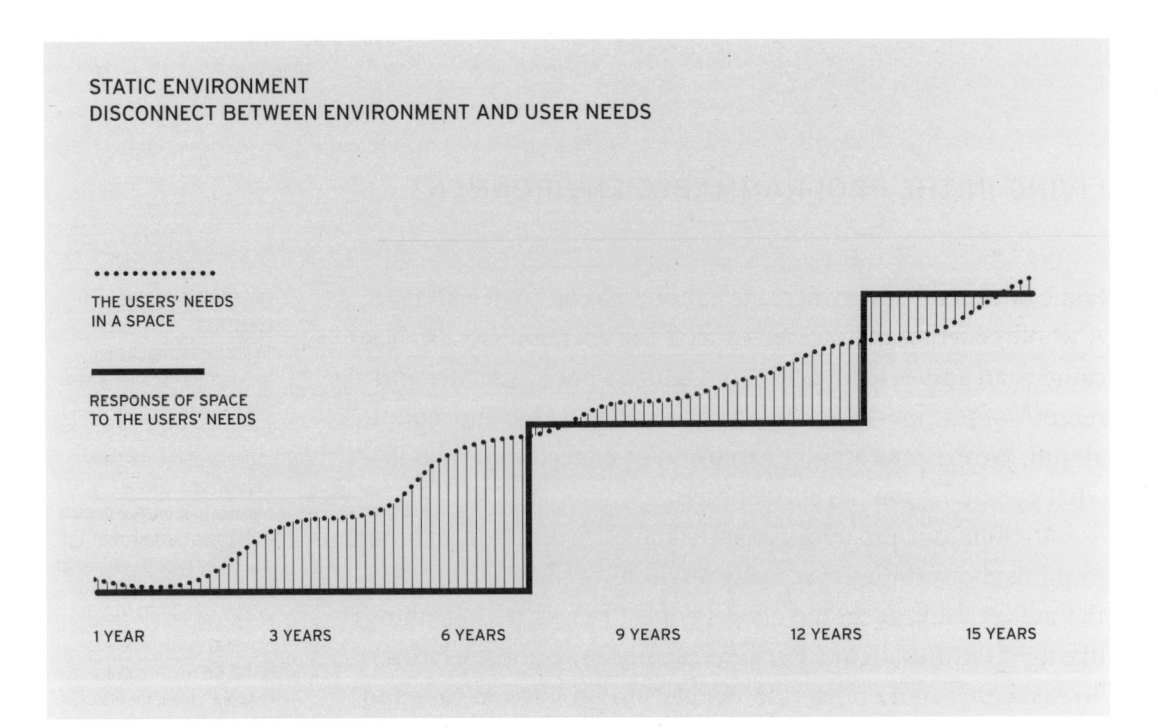

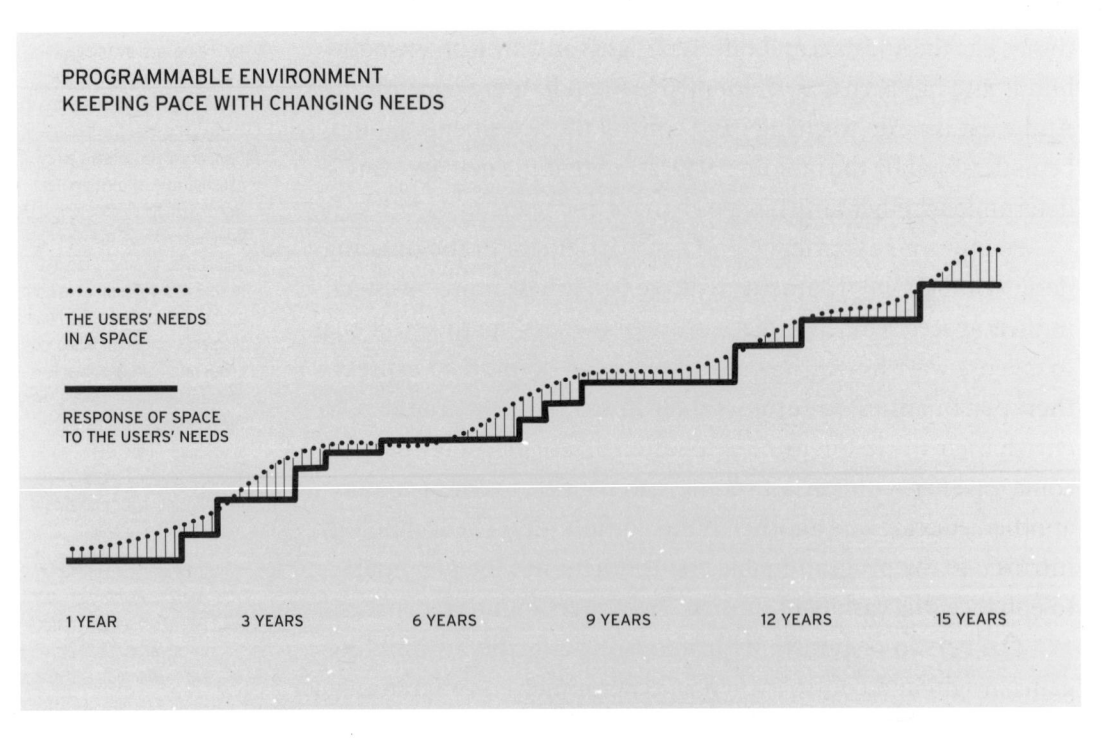

••••••••••••
THE USERS' NEEDS
IN A SPACE

──────────
RESPONSE OF SPACE
TO THE USERS' NEEDS

1 YEAR   3 YEARS   6 YEARS   9 YEARS   12 YEARS   15 YEARS

A CLOSER MATCH TO USER NEEDS
In the traditional model, an environment grows further and further disconnected from the needs of the people who use it, until a major renovation is completed for a temporary improvement in alignment. In the programmable environment, ongoing changes in the environment enable it to more closely match current user needs throughout the building life cycle.

LIVING IN THE PROGRAMMABLE ENVIRONMENT

Some of us remember when a telephone was only a telephone. A whole generation, however, expects the telephone to also be a camera, an answering machine, an address book, a sender and receiver of text messages or e-mails, a web browser, and a photo album. We expect a similar explosion of expectations about what's possible from an environment.

At minimum, programmability should free people from having to think about things that really ought to be able to think for themselves. Next, it should allow people to easily relocate things like light fixtures, light switches, receptacles, and projectors. To make that more powerful, people should have an easy and intuitive way to make and break control relationships between things like thermostats and diffusers, lights and switches, window blinds and light sensors, space dividers and lighting controls. And what they do to change and control those elements should be understood by the building at large, so that the manager can determine whether larger-scale changes are needed.

People who experience and can participate in the ongoing design of their environments will, we believe, be more invested in their spaces. They will feel a sense of ownership; they will begin to explore ways in which environments can do more to express their personalities, to support their interactions with others, to enrich their work. Environments, after all, are places for people to come together—to transact business, to politick, to entertain one another, educate one another, build community. The technology intrinsic to the programmable environment has the potential to enhance this variety of human encounters in interior spaces.

The person responsible for managing a facility or building gains insight and control; when an environment is programmable, all of its parts and systems operate as one network rather than individual components. Data on building parameters like energy utilization, use and occupancy, and the frequency of change, combined with tools for analysis and reporting, give the manager tools to reduce costs and increase the performance of the building for the people who use it.

SWARMING BUILDING ELEMENTS

"In the Digital Revolution… architecture becomes a game played by its users. And not only architecture will be subject to the forces of real-time calculation. Planning, construction, interior design, and landscape design are also ready to be developed as real-time games. During the design process the game is designed by the architect and played by all parties involved. During the life cycle of the building and the built environment, the game is played by their users, by the visitors, and by the built environment itself…. By playing the game the participants set the parameters. Each actor triggers an array of sensors writing the new data into a database, from where the building picks up the new data and starts reconfiguring itself, in shape, in content, or in both shape and content….The building elements consist of numerous cooperating programmable elements, behaving like a swarm. The building elements will show flocking behavior, always keeping an eye on the neighboring actor and always ready to act and react."

—Introduction to Game Set and Match, an international and interdisciplinary conference sponsored by Delft University of Technology and directed by Kas Oosterhuis

Because in a well-designed programmable environment the location, programming, relocation, and reprogramming of sensors is a simple, everyday activity, the manager can fine-tune the information that she's receiving as the use of the building changes. And by having a multi-dimensional picture, through historical data, of the effect of changes made over time, the manager can continuously experiment, learn, and apply that learning to the operation of the environment.

The payoff from this kind of approach is enormous, and both short- and long-term. In the short-term, the people using the building have more control—whether they're concentrating in a workstation, meeting in an auditorium, or trying to reduce energy consumption across an entire campus. In the long-term, the building can change and adapt to a new purpose for a new group of people, reducing their costs and eliminating the environmental impact of a conventional renovation or reconstruction. And in between, the programmable building easily accommodates a reorganized department, a repurposed room, or three tenants instead of two. The result is sustainability—of purpose and usefulness for both the people currently using a building and the owner of the building over a longer term.

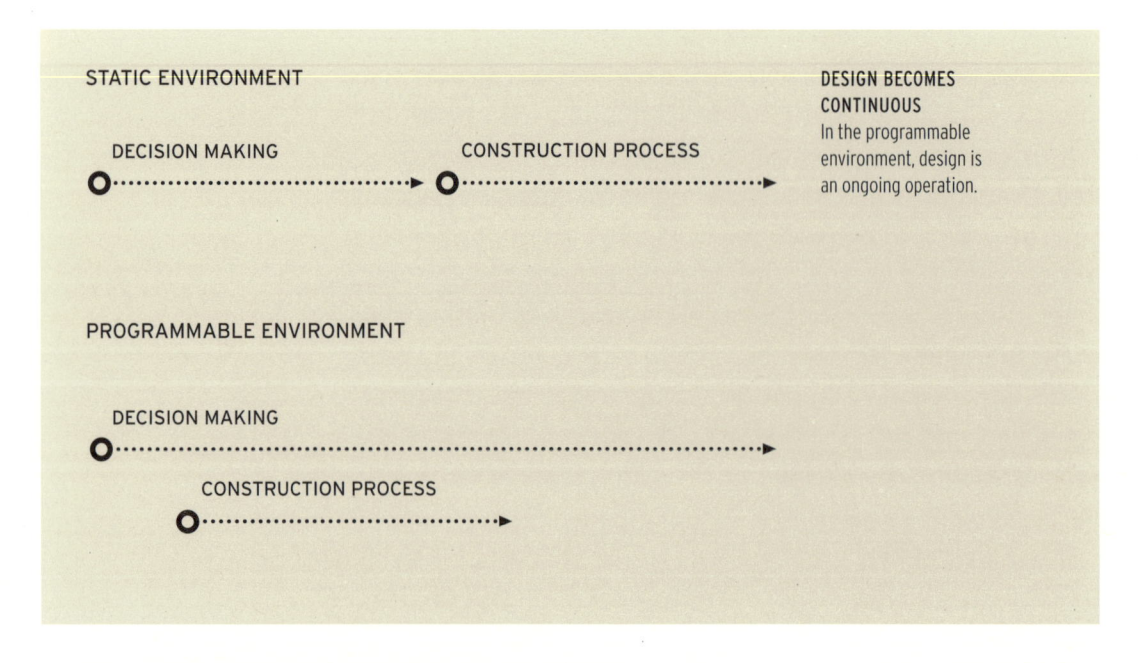

STATIC ENVIRONMENT

DECISION MAKING   CONSTRUCTION PROCESS

DESIGN BECOMES CONTINUOUS
In the programmable environment, design is an ongoing operation.

PROGRAMMABLE ENVIRONMENT

DECISION MAKING

CONSTRUCTION PROCESS

AHEAD: DESIGNING IN ANTICIPATION OF CHANGE

In 1968, Robert Propst and the Herman Miller Research Corporation brought systems thinking to furnishing commercial offices. To address the rapidly rising demand for office space fueled by the developing computer industry and the emergent information economy, they proposed a new kind of product called Action Office®.

Propst and his team described what proved to be a disruptive innovation in interior design and space planning. They set in motion a series of complementary investments and initiatives that soon cast a new industry. The advent of office systems precipitated new capital, new competitors, new offers, new professions, and new ways to think about the design of commercial space.

We believe that the concept of programmable environments will incite change on a similar scale. There is much to be done, and we believe it is best done participatively, inclusively, so that adaptation happens fastest where it's valued most. We expect to be surprised by where the path ahead takes us, as new practices emerge, people work across disciplines, technology develops, and building users become adept at co-design.

The performance of the built environment has long been measured according to the same attributes: iconic status, security, comfort, efficiency. The importance of human performance—enabling people to meet their potential—and the demand for global sustainability make clear that these measures are no longer enough. Places that succeed in the twenty-first century will be based on adaptability.

The promise of technology—especially when intrinsic to building materials—makes this new paradigm possible and makes clear the path forward. It is possible to design a spatial experience to be continuously designed by others, in anticipation of changes not yet imagined. Buildings need no longer stand outside of time, impervious to the needs of the people who use them.

We have made a beginning, but we count on insight and contribution from you, agents of change in architecture, engineering, and design, as we transform how buildings are designed, built, managed, and used—a transformation to "always building" environments.

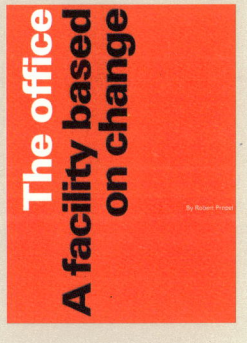

Published in 1968, this book outlined the principles of a new approach to furnishing commercial office spaces.

FURTHER READING

This eclectic collection of books, articles, and websites influenced the development of our ideas. We owe a debt of gratitude to all of these authors, website creators, and many more from whom we learned and whose thinking served to test our ideas.

We invite you to join in understanding both the issues and the potential, and in the creation of the programmable environment. We will keep our reading list current at www.HermanMiller.com/AlwaysBuilding.

On Innovation
These readings were important to the genesis of our work. They provided insight into new ways of thinking about innovation in the built environment.

Axelrod, Robert, and Michael D. Cohen. *Harnessing Complexity: Organizational Implications of a Scientific Frontier.* New York: Free Press, 1999.

Brand, Stewart. *The Clock of the Long Now: Time and Responsibility.* New York: Basic Books, 1999.

Fox, Michael A. "Beyond Kinetic." Massachusetts Institute of Technology, Department of Architecture, 2001. Full paper. http://kdg.mit.edu/Pdf/beyond.pdf.

Gershenfeld, Neil A. *When Things Start to Think.* New York: Henry Holt, 1999.

Horgen, Turid H., Michael L. Joroff, William L. Porter, and Donald A. Schön. *Excellence by Design: Transforming Workplace and Work Practice.* New York: John Wiley and Sons, 1999.

Kennedy, Sheila, ed. *Bugs, Fish, Floors & Ceilings: Luminous Bodies and the Contemporary Problem of Material Presence: A Catalog of Student Work.* Cambridge: Harvard University Graduate School of Design, 2000.

On Sustainability
All of the readings in some way connect to ideas about sustainability, but a few address the point directly.

Addington, Michelle. "No Building Is an Island: A Look at the Different Scales of Energy." *Harvard Design Magazine* 26 (spring/summer 2007): 38-45.

Gore, Al. *An Inconvenient Truth: The Planetary Emergency of Global Warming and What We Can Do About It.* Emmaus, PA: Rodale, 2006.

Green Building SmartMarket Report: 2006. New York: McGraw-Hill Construction, 2005. http://construction.ecnext.com/coms2/summary_0249-87264_ITM_analytics

Robertson, Ross. "A Brighter Shade of Green: How Radical Innovation Is Transforming Environmentalism." *What Is Enlightenment?* 38 (October/December 2007): 41-62

Steffen, Alex, ed. *World Changing: A User's Guide for the 21st Century.* New York: Harry N. Abrams, 2006.

"Termite-inspired Air Conditioning." Biomimicry Institute, Missoula, MT. Case Study. http://www.biomimicryinstitute.org/case-studies/case-studies/termite-inspired-air-conditioning.html

Worldchanging. Alex Steffen and Jamais Cascio, founders. Global nonprofit media collaborative dedicated to exploring tools, models, and ideas for building a better future. http://www.worldchanging.com.

On Architecture and Design

There is always an active conversation in the architecture and design world about the meaning and purpose of the built environment. These readings represent a particular leading edge in the discussion, exploring change and the role of digital technology in the built environment.

Buxton, Bill. *Sketching User Experiences: Getting the Design Right and the Right Design.* San Francisco: Morgan Kaufmann, 2007.

Greenfield, Adam, and Mark Shepard. *Situated Technologies Pamphlet 1: Urban Computing and its Discontents.* New York: Architectural League of New York, 2007.

Kaspori, Dennis. "A Communism of Ideas: Towards an Architectural Open Source Practice." Maze Corporation, Standplaats, NL. Publication. http://www.themaze.org/opensource.html.

Kronenburg, Robert. *Flexible: Architecture That Responds to Change.* London: Laurence King, 2007.

McCullough, Malcolm. *Digital Ground: Architecture, Pervasive Computing, and Environmental Knowing.* Cambridge: MIT Press, 2005.

National Institute of Building Sciences. "United States National Building Information Modeling Standard (version 1, part 1)." Facility Information Council, 2007. Publication. http://www.facilityinformationcouncil.org/bim/publications.php

Oosterhuis, Kas. *Hyperbodies: Towards an E-motive Architecture.* Basel, Switzerland: Birkhäuser, 2003.

Open Architecture Network. http://www.openarchitecturenetwork.org. Online, open-source community dedicated to improving living conditions through innovative and sustainable design.

Senagala, Mahesh. "Kinetic, Responsive and Adaptive: A Complex-Adaptive Approach to Smart Architecture." In *Proceedings of SIGRADI International Conference.* Lima, Peru, 2005.

Sterling, Bruce. *Shaping Things.* Cambridge: MIT Press, 2005.

Studio Wikitecture. http://www.studiowikitecture.com/home.php5. On-line community exploring whether mass collaboration, collective intelligence, and open-source paradigm can improve the quality of architecture and urban planning.

On Technology in Buildings

These readings explore some of the key issues in the implementation of technology in buildings. They are generally from the perspective of energy savings, which is the predominant reason for introducing digital technology and automated systems. There is a clear but indirect connection to the green build movement.

Bowen, Ted Smalley. "Overly Smart Buildings." *Technology Research News* (April 20/27, 2005). http://trnmag.com/Stories/2005/042005/Impact_Assessment_--_Overly_smart_buildings_042005.html.

Brambley, M.R., P. Haves, S.C. McDonald, P. Torcellini, D. Hansen, D.R. Holmberg, and K.W. Roth. "Advanced Sensors and Controls for Building Applications: Market Assessment and Potential R&D Pathways." Battelle Pacific Northwest National Laboratory for U.S. Department of Energy, Office of Building Technology, 2005. Report. http://www.eere.energy.gov/buildings/highperformance/commercial_analysis.html

Direct Digital Controls. Iowa Energy Center, Iowa State University. http://www.ddc-online.org/. Provides unbiased information on DDC and searchable guide to DDC manufacturers.

Energy Information Administration. U.S. Department of Energy. http://www.eia.doe.gov/emeu/cbecs. Provides policy-neutral data, forecasts, and analyses to promote sound policy making, efficient markets, and public understanding regarding energy and its interaction with the economy and the environment.

Green Building SmartMarket Report: 2006. New York: McGraw-Hill Construction, 2005. http://construction.ecnext.com/coms2/summary_0249-87264_ITM_analytics

"High-Performance Commercial Buildings: A Technology Roadmap." U.S. Department of Energy, Office of Building Technology, 2000. Publication. http://www.eere.energy.gov/buildings/info/documents/pdfs/roadmap_lowres.pdf.

Institute for the Future. "Technology Horizons Program SR1042." Palo Alto: 2007. http://www.iftf.org/research/technology.html. Independent nonprofit research group that helps companies look beyond technical feasibility to identify the value in new technologies, forecast adoption and diffusion patterns, and discover new market opportunities and threats.

Roth, Kurt W., Detlef Westphalen, Michael Y. Feng, Patricia Llana, and Louis Quartararo. "Energy Impact of Commercial Building Controls and Performance Diagnostics: Market Characterization, Energy Impact of Building Faults and Energy Savings Potential." TIAX, LLC., for U.S. Department of Energy, Office of Building Technology, 2005. Report. http://www.eere.energy.gov/buildings/highperformance/commercial_analysis.html

Russell, Daniel M., Norbert A. Streitz, and Terry Winograd. "Building Disappearing Computers." Communications of the ACM 48, no. 3 (2005): 42-48.

SENSEable City Laboratory. http://senseable.mit.edu/. Research initiative at MIT that studies the impact of new technologies on cities.

Implications of the Spread of Digital Technology

These writings illustrate some of the many implications of the growing diffusion of digital technology into all aspects of society.

Bradsher, Keith. "An Opportunity for Wall St. in China's Surveillance Boom." *New York Times* (September 11, 2007). http://www.nytimes.com/2007/09/11/business/worldbusiness/11security.html?_r=1&dlbk&oref=slogin

Brinkley, Ian. "Defining the Knowledge Economy." The Work Foundation, 2006. Research paper. http://www.theworkfoundation.com

Cairncross, Frances. *The Death of Distance: How the Communications Revolution Is Changing Our Lives.* Rev. ed. Boston: Harvard Business School Press, 2001.

Center for Virtual Architecture. http://cva.ap.buffalo.edu. Explores the possibilities offered by computational systems for rethinking human interaction with (and within) the built environment.

Erickson, Thomas, and David W. McDonald, ed. *HCI Remixed: Reflections on Works That Have Influenced the HCI Community.* Cambridge: Massachusetts Institute of Technology, 2008.

Ganz, John F., et al. "The Expanding Digital Universe: A Forecast of Worldwide Information Growth through 2010." IDC for EMC Corp., 2007. White paper. [This paper has been updated (March 2008). "The Diverse and Exploding Digital Universe: A Forecast of Worldwide Information Growth through 2011." Links on the EMC website take you to this newest publication.]

Greenfield, Adam. *Everyware: The Dawning Age of Ubiquitous Computing.* Berkeley: New Riders Publishing, 2006.

Igoe, Tom. *Making Things Talk.* Sebastopol: O'Reilly, 2007.

Maeda, John. *Creative Code.* New York: Thames & Hudson, 2004.

Media Architecture Group. Gernot Tscherteu and Wolfgang Leeb. http://www.mediaarchitecture.org/ Established in 2006 to initiate a discourse on new phenomena of media facades and architecture.

Reconfigurable House. Usman Hague and Adam Somlai-Fischer, builders. http://house.propositions.org.uk/. Website featuring an environment constructed from thousands of low tech components that can be "rewired" by visitors.

New Ways of Building and Lean Construction

The website of the Lean Construction Institute (http://www.leanconstruction.org) states: "We do research to develop knowledge regarding project based production management in the design, engineering, and construction of capital facilities." These readings are a sample of that research.

Ballard, Glenn. "Lean Project Delivery System: LCI White Paper-8." Lean Construction Institute, 2006. White paper. http://www.leanconstruction.org/

Ballard, Glenn, and Greg Howell. "What Kind of Production is Construction?" In *Proceedings of the 6th Annual Conference of the International Group for Lean Construction, IGLC-6.* Guaruja, Brazil, 1998. http://www.ce.berkeleyedu/~tommelein/IGLC-6/index.html

Bertelsen, Sven, and Rafael Sacks. "Towards a New Understanding of the Construction Industry and the Nature of its Production." In *Proceedings of the 15th Annual Conference of the International Group for Lean Construction, IGLC-15.* East Lansing, Michigan, 2007. http://www.iglc.net/conferences/2007/folder.2007-06-29.2095743756/

Building Futures Institute, Ball State University. http://www.bsu.edu/web/capweb/bfi/. Conducts research on open building, computational methods, building culture, innovative practices, and design theory and methods.

Cuperus, Ype. "An Introduction to Open Building." In *Proceedings of the 9th Annual Conference of the International Group for Lean Construction, IGLC-9.* Singapore, 2001. http://www.iglc.net/conferences/2001/Papers/

International Council for Research and Innovation in Building and Construction. Working Commission W104: Open Building Implementation. http://www.open-building.org. Network of researchers and practitioners who seek to formulate theories about the built environment and develop methods of design and building construction compatible with the Open Building approach.

Koskela, Laurie, and Ruben Vrijhoef. "The Prevalent Theory of Construction is a Hindrance for Innovation." In *Proceedings of the 8th Annual Conference of the International Group for Lean Construction, IGLC-9.* Brighton, UK, 2000. http://www.iglc.net/conferences/2000/Papers/.

Open Buildings Strategic Studies. Ype Cuperus, director. http://www.obom.org. International network of Open Building experts, committed to finding the best solutions for transformations in the built environment.

Rooke, John, Lauri Koskela, Sven Bertelsen, and Guilherme Henrich. "Centred Flows: A Lean Approach to Decision Making and Organisation." In *Proceedings of the 15th Annual Conference of the International Group for Lean Construction, IGLC-15.* East Lansing, Michigan, 2007. http://www.iglc.net/conferences/2007/folder.2007-06-29.2095743756/

ABOUT THE AUTHORS

Jim Long is an engineer and researcher at Herman Miller. He has spent the past 20 years working on new solutions for the problems of built environments.

Jennifer Magnolfi is an architect and technologist whose research explores the intersection among architecture, interaction design, and building systems.

Lois Maassen, who edited this book, has long advanced communications, research and development, and technology programs for Herman Miller.

As we have collaborated on this project, we have come to see ourselves as analogous to the inclusive, multi-disciplinary teams required to envision the programmable environment. Each of us represents a different perspective and depth of distinct professional knowledge and experience; together we can create something that none of us could have created alone.

Communications consulting and graphic design by People Design, Grand Rapids, Michigan (www.PeopleDesign.com)

Illustrations by James Gulliver Hancock and Jody Williams

Photography © Barrett, Hedrich Blessing, page 58

Architecture by OWP/P, page 58

® **HermanMiller**, ◎, and Action Office are among
the trademarks of Herman Miller, Inc.

™Convia is among the trademarks of Herman Miller, Inc.

O.KN2704

Contact Herman Miller through www.HermanMiller.com
or HMConvia.com or by calling (800) 851 1196